I0092254

THE JUSTICE LABORATORY

INSIGHTS

CRITICAL THINKING ON INTERNATIONAL AFFAIRS

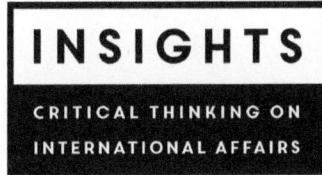

Providing new perspectives and knowledge on an increasingly complex, uncertain, and interconnected world.

The Chatham House Insights Series
Series Editor: Caroline Soper

The Insights series provides new perspectives on and knowledge about an increasingly complex, uncertain, and interconnected world. Concise, lively, and authoritative, these books explore, through different modes of interpretation, a wide range of country, regional, and international developments, all within a global context. Focusing on topical issues in key policy areas, such as health, security, economics, law, and the environment, volumes in the series will be written accessibly by leading experts—both academic and practitioner—to anticipate trends and illuminate new ideas and thinking. Insights books will be of great interest to all those seeking to develop a deeper understanding of the policy challenges and choices facing decision-makers, including academics, practitioners, and general readers.

Published or forthcoming titles:

Chatham House, the Royal Institute of International Affairs, is a world-leading policy institute based in London. Its mission is to help governments and societies build a sustainably secure, prosperous, and just world.

Chatham House does not express opinions of its own. The opinions expressed in this publication are the responsibility of the author(s).

THE
JUSTICE
LABORATORY

International Law in Africa

KERSTIN BREE CARLSON

BROOKINGS INSTITUTION PRESS
Washington, D.C.

CHATHAM HOUSE
The Royal Institute of International Affairs
London

Copyright © 2022
THE BROOKINGS INSTITUTION
1775 Massachusetts Avenue, N.W.
Washington, D.C. 20036
www.brookings.edu

All rights reserved. No part of this publication may be reproduced
or transmitted in any form or by any means without permission
in writing from the Brookings Institution Press.

The Brookings Institution is a private nonprofit organization devoted to research,
education, and publication on important issues of domestic and foreign policy. Its
principal purpose is to bring the highest quality independent research and analysis
to bear on current and emerging policy problems. Interpretations or conclusions in
Brookings publications should be understood to be solely those of the authors.

Library of Congress Control Number: 2021953042

ISBN 9780815738138 (pbk)
ISBN 9780815738145 (ebook)

9 8 7 6 5 4 3 2 1

Typeset in Adobe Garamond

Composition by Elliott Beard

For Uncle Rik, our cheerleader

Contents

Acknowledgments

The book you are holding in your hands is the fruit of years of questions, conversations, ideas, challenges, and encouragement, and it owes many debts.

Mikael Rask Madsen of iCourts, University of Copenhagen, encouraged me to pursue academic passions, not just practicalities. Sten Rynning at the Center for War Studies, University of Southern Denmark (SDU), and Caroline Soper of Chatham House invited me to think about how I might present international criminal law outside of a law or politics classroom. Susan Perry at the American University of Paris (AUP) organized yearly study trips to international courts in The Hague and made a place for me. Malcolm Feeley, Kristen Luker, Martin Shapiro, Ronelle Alexander, Steven Bundy, the late David Caron, and the Honorable David Folsom shaped my approach to thinking and writing about law and how it impacts society.

In 2013 the Africa Research Service (ARS) of the U.S. State Department sent me to Addis Ababa to address the African Union regarding the International Criminal Court (ICC); this opportunity to engage in real-world politics forever changed my consideration of the institution and how we should talk about it. As the rapporteur for the 2016 Brandeis Institute on International Judiciary at iCourts, I was a fly on the wall as twenty international judges discussed their institutions and the field, a singular and extraordinary experience; I am also grateful to Henrik Stampe Lund for his counsel regarding how to fulfill my rapporteur role.

Research in Dakar from 2016 to 2018 was supported by iCourts, the Danish National Research Foundation, and SDU. Trips to Addis Ababa, Ethiopia, and Arusha, Tanzania, in 2019 were financed by the Dreyer's Fund and the Schaeffer Center for the Study of Genocide, Human Rights, and Conflict Prevention; these funders made my fieldwork possible. Likewise, I am thankful for the intellectual rigor and curiosity of my colleagues at SDU and our Masters of International Security and Law students, where I have shopped and developed many of these ideas.

My collaboration with Sharon Weill (AUP) and Kim Thuy Seelinger (Washington University in St. Louis) regarding the Habré trial and its impact generated much of the empirical material I draw on in chapter 3. Our co-edited book, *The President on Trial: Prosecuting Hissène Habré* (Oxford University Press, 2020), is the fruit of years of joint interviews, conversations, and imaginings; they are a dream team. Thank you to Olivier Schmitt and Mathew Ford, and other participants in a European International Studies Association (EISA) 2018 panel on external and internal dynamics for helpful comments on an early version of the Rwanda chapter. Julius Maina at *The Conversation* has invited me to contribute on the ICC, Habré, and other topics over the years, developing both my approach and writing clarity. Thanks to Shahla Ali and participants in the alternative dispute resolution conference in Hong Kong in February 2019 and the Transitional Justice pre-conference to EUROCRIM in September 2019 for helpful comments on the South Sudan chapter; thanks too to Nicki Kindersley for her generosity in sharing ideas and a critical eye. Astrid Jamar and participants in the European Conference on African Studies (ECAS), and their Third World Approaches to International Law (TWAIL) scholarship, pushed forward my thinking regarding the Rwanda, Habré, and Arusha chapters.

Experts and practitioners in Arusha, Dakar, Addis Ababa, and Juba generously shared their knowledge and perspectives with me. Martin Mennecke neutralized the better angels of his nature to offer comments on the ICC chapter. The three anonymous reviewers who strengthened the manuscript while simultaneously conferring their enthusiasm for the project are very appreciated. Line Engbo Gissel has chewed over many of these ideas across the kitchen table and in planes, trains, and automobiles over several years, and this book is better for it. Lin Adrian, Zuzanna Godsmirska, Jakob von Holtermann, Cary Hollingshead-Strick, and Anne-Lise Kjær helped me scale the last steps of the mountain with our scheduled writing sessions.

My family and friends have made this work possible. Sam and Alice taught me French, which opened a window to Africa. The Carlsons, Ragones, MacIntyres, Brodersen-Schiønnings, Torts, and Cornells, as well as Bojana, Brennan, Carly, Cary, Eileen, Jackie, Josh, Kim, Laura, Mel and Todd, Peter, Ray-Ray, Serena, Susanna, and Tamara, are always ready for a chat, a laugh, or a commiseration. Claudio checked all the equations. An urban village cared for my children (and me!) as I traveled for research and conferences related to this work: Alice, Anu and Dhiraj, Amalia and Christian, Amanda and Julia, Chiaki and Don, Amy and Bjørn, Andrea and Ian, Ayako and Jan, Bea, Brooke, Clara, Claudio, Diana, Greta and Jon, Jake and Laura, James, Jasna and Raul, Jed, Jenna and Jin, Caro and Stu, Jette and Michael, Juanan, Katharina, Karen and Kasper, Kim, Laura and Etan, Emma and Steve, Lena, Lisbeth and Jan, Mom and Dad, Mor and Far—thank you.

The children in question have almost always submitted to the bohemian messiness of these arrangements with excellent cheer: Lolo and Niamh, I'm so glad to share this journey with you.

Copenhagen
November 2021

Introduction

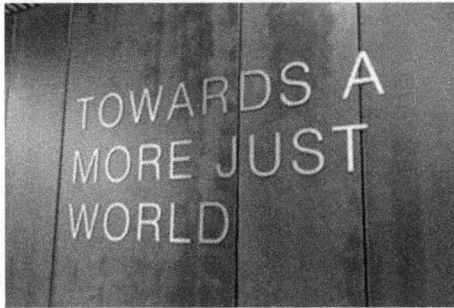

Are law and norms exportable and can they prevent state-sponsored atrocity? This is the goal of the international criminal justice project. From early experiments like the postwar Nuremberg and Tokyo tribunals to the recent United Nations tribunals for Rwanda and Yugoslavia, new institutional forms have aimed to define and enforce core human rights in order to limit human suffering. This project reached its pinnacle with the creation of the International Criminal Court (ICC), a membership-based international organization founded in 2002 and empowered to try individuals from member countries accused of breaching core human rights, that is, committing genocide, crimes against humanity, war crimes, and, since 2018, "aggression." The ICC's goal is nothing less than a "more just world," as the plaque at its headquarters in The Hague, Netherlands, proclaims. Proponents of the ICC see it as a critical turning point after centuries of state-sponsored atrocities; it is the institution that will push the decades' long "justice cascade"[1] of heightened awareness of and respect for human rights to global fruition.

Twenty-two years after the Rome Statute (1998) crafted the future ICC, the international criminal justice project is fragmented and contested. The ad hoc tribunals for Rwanda and Yugoslavia have closed. Similarly, ambitious hybrid local/international tribunals—smaller, cheaper, and more easily managed by local power holders—have sprung up as the venue of choice for adjudicating state-sponsored violence or ongoing intractable conflict. The ICC is locked in opposition with what might euphemistically be called its client base (Sub-Saharan Africa, from which nearly all ICC jurisprudence arises), because the African Union makes annual calls for its members to quit the court. World powers that never came on board at the ICC's founding, such as the United States, China, India, and Russia, remain unenthusiastic about the court, or worse.[2] Perhaps most catastrophically for the international criminal justice project, even the ICC's "sure bet" countries—western Europe and Canada—have grown lukewarm in support, evidenced by the tepid reaction that greeted the 2018 addition of a new crime to the ICC's crime base—aggression.[3] Intellectual capital is diminishing in lockstep with political capital, because human rights and transitional justice are increasingly lumped together with other failing neoliberal governance conceptions such as the recently abandoned Washington consensus. For all its utopian design, the international criminal justice project is foundering amid disappearing funding, heightened skepticism, and decreasing credibility regarding the social impact it can deliver.

Genocide, crimes against humanity, and war crimes are universally renounced state behaviors. Law is a trellis for good governance. Given the universal recognition of the *what* (no acceptance of state atrocity crimes) and the *how* (rule of law, practiced by courts, leading to criminal punishment), how are we to explain the declining star power of international criminal justice? In *The Justice Laboratory* I examine select jurisprudence from five international justice institutions extant or in development across Africa to answer this question. The bulk of *The Justice Laboratory* explores cases examined by international criminal justice institutions: the ICC in chapter 1, the UN's Rwanda tribunal in chapter 2, the hybrid tribunal that tried Chadian dictator Hissène Habré in chapter 3, and the hybrid tribunal proposed for South Sudan through its fragile peace agreement in chapter 4. These institutions differ in design but share similar deficits as regards the capacity for law to "speak truth to power." Instead of rule-of-law practice, the jurisprudence (in the case of the first three) and design (in the case of the fourth, since it is not yet operational) of these institutions suggest that they have been captured by political interests. The final chapter of the book examines the East African Court of Justice, a reconstituted trade court in Arusha, Tanzania, that is inventively pushing the boundaries of how courts constrain states and drawing lessons from other international courts in the process. This final chapter, together with the book's conclusion, considers how emerging or proposed African institutions embody governance possibilities that are promised, but so far not delivered, by international criminal tribunals.

No region has felt the burden of liberal rule-of-law exports like Sub-Saharan Africa. From the UN Tribunal for Rwanda to hybrid tribunals in Sierra Leone, Senegal, and the Central African Republic, to nearly the entirety of the ICC's practice, Africa has been the locus to see if the law can constrain political violence. The practice and potential for international or supranational law to constrain state action is being reinvented in numerous institutions across Africa. This book visits several sites, considering with each chapter a legal problem particular to the institution scrutinized. Through snapshots offered from within the five institutional examples, *The Justice Laboratory* seeks to open elements of the "black box" of law. It does so by applying an empirical sociolegal method that shows how jurisprudence and legal practice provide important entry points to understand the political dynamics of international courts.

Appropriation and Experimentation: International Criminal Justice in Africa

The story of African challenges to international criminal justice is not a story of African backwardness, savagery, or ineptitude, although it is sometimes told that way. Rather, the central story of international criminal justice in Africa is a story of local political savvy, and in this respect, it is a story that looks much like political savvy anywhere in the world; there is nothing particularly "African" about it. In Africa, as chapters 1 and 2 discuss, local political interests have instrumentalized both the ICC and the ad hoc UN International Criminal Tribunal for Rwanda (ICTR). Local political appropriation is unexpected given that the value of these international institutions is their purported inoculation against local politics. In the case of state-sponsored atrocity, it is local political interest that usually must be overcome in the transition to liberal state practice; this is where a neutral, objective, uninvolved arbiter trying and punishing violators of international criminal law promises the most benefit. There are many losses of efficiency in placing local actors before an international institution: translation, staging (travel), and historical and factual familiarity and comprehension are all rendered more difficult by transporting a case out of its locale to be heard by a foreign body. The result should be an objectivity arising from an institution willing and able to pronounce truth uninhibited by its potential unpopularity.

In the case of hybrid tribunals, which operate under a non-uniform mixture of national and international law and actors, local power politics also play a role. This is less surprising, given that connection to local practices and knowledge is part of the appeal of hybrid institutions. In Africa hybrid tribunals have been set up in Sierra Leone and Senegal and are under development in the Central African Republic and South Sudan. Hybrid tribunals are becoming increasingly popular as international criminal justice institutions, largely due to their lower cost and more precise jurisdictional mandate. Hybrid tribunals can be designed to capture specific crimes within a limited time period, as is the case with the hybrid Chambres Africaines Extraordinaires (CAE) in Senegal, the subject of chapter 3. The CAE had jurisdiction over atrocities committed in Chad between 1982 and 1990, the precise period of Hissène Habré's rule. Given the precision of its mandate, when the CAE issued an indictment, and ultimately a judgment, against Habré, no one could feign surprise. The jurisdictional limitations of the CAE mitigated any danger that it might broaden its consideration to capture modern illiberal rule in Chad; this effectively protected Idriss Déby, the autocrat who ousted Habré in a coup in 1990 and went on to employ several of Habré's associates and techniques to maintain his rule over Chad for the past thirty years.[4] The appropriation of hybrid tribunals is thus often seen in their very structure, with limitations on their mandate permitting investigation of only a certain kind of violation committed by a certain political affiliate, instead of a more general, and therefore objective, construction.

What is perhaps unexpected from the local political appropriation of international criminal justice institutions is the cooperation by the institutions themselves, which have also found their own interests met by this instrumentalization. Successful local appropriation thus impacts the "truth" international criminal justice institutions speak when speaking truth to power. International criminal justice institutions produce legal doctrine governing the condemnation of state-sponsored atrocity, and appropriation of international justice institutions in service to local political interests impacts the doctrinal allocutions of those institutions. Through examples that explore how the evolution of certain legal doctrines are party to extra-legal interests, this book examines some unexpected ways that local power politics substantially influence the course and content of international jurisprudence, whose outcome is usually unacknowledged by the institutions practicing international justice.

Transitional Justice, Backlash, and New Ideas

European and North American democracies following the rule of law have enjoyed several uninterrupted decades of economic and cultural preeminence.[5] Rule-of-law norms, particularly as regards human rights, are credited with ensuring these countries' improvement-oriented relationships between government and citizenry. As the kernel of western liberalism and good governance, law and norms have also functioned as the preferred instrument of rehabilitation for authoritarian states. Beginning in the 1990s, a burgeoning international criminal law practice sought to address the worst infractions of authoritarian states by putting individuals on trial for violations of core rights (genocide, crimes against humanity, and war crimes). International criminal law thus joined constitutional consultation, human rights articulation, and civil society support in the arsenal of legal mechanisms to develop good governance in states understood to be "transitioning" from autocracy to democracy. The tools used to assist states in this transition were grouped under the heading "transitional justice," a field that included courts, truth commissions, lustration campaigns, and amnesties as mechanisms to heal societies riven by conflict. Transitional justice is discussed at length in chapter 4.

After thirty years of practice, however, it is not clear that the experimental application of international criminal law has made much headway in transforming rights-violating states into rights-respecting states. We find continued authoritarianism and ethnic nationalism in states for which international criminal tribunals were constructed. Moreover, international criminal justice has proven itself susceptible to local political appropriation, weakening its claim to provide apolitical legal formulations.

These observations have contributed to the pushback against international courts that characterizes the current discourse. This growing resistance extends beyond African "backlash,"[6] and includes skepticism of supranational governance in even the most traditionally committed quarters, for example, Europe, with Brexit being one obvious example. The case of African resistance to international criminal justice institutions merits particular attention for two central reasons. First, African resistance to international justice is distinguishable from other forms of pushback evidenced in the modern populist era because it is not a pushback subsequent to adherence or adoption: it is all pushback. Other international legal institutions have had adherents prior to defectors. The story of international criminal justice across Africa shows serial examples where would-be adherents instrumentalized institutions for recognizable political gain, rather than internalizing the norms or practices of those institutions.

This instrumentalization distinguishes the African experience from others' and brings us to the second reason to consider African backlash, which is that there is demonstrable value in supranational judicial governance. Supranational legal formulations remain a tested and reliable means by which to balance short-term political exigencies—what de Tocqueville termed the "tyranny of the majority"—within domestic political markets.[7] There is plenty of self-interested good sense in the decisions that states make when they choose to limit their sovereignty and flexibility to make determinations domestically by engaging international obligations, the political equivalent of "paying it forward." In other words, to paraphrase Churchill's summary of democracy, while international courts are imperfect, they are often still the best means of achieving states' justice goals. This means that even if African leaders reject supranational institutions as neocolonial, neoliberal, or on other grounds, it is still a mistake to reject supranational governance because it can bring demonstrable political gains to the countries that institute it.

By many accounts, the twenty-first century will belong to Africa. The massive colonial fingerprint of western nations—resource extraction and norm exportation—that characterized the nineteenth and twentieth centuries is challenged by the rising BRICS nations (Brazil, Russia, India, China, and South Africa). BRICS nations extract and invest but do not condition aid on human rights or good governance. Meanwhile, African nations are defining themselves in the current post-postcolonial era, sometimes progressively rewriting governance dictates (South Africa's Truth and Reconciliation Commission; Thomas Sankara's Burkina Faso) and challenging global power structures and their related governance assumptions as they do. What sort of governance will characterize the continent, and how will rule-of-law principles factor in?

International Law for Non-Jurists

The Justice Laboratory examines attempts to exert rule-of-law constraints on political violence. On its face, law is an unlikely tool to defeat state-sponsored violence. First, law is often a form of state-sponsored violence; even the most highly functioning democracies are built on structural inequalities that are further enforced by law.[8] Second, law's most significant addition to governance is arguably in the realm of ideas. Rights are key examples of law's ideological domain; when someone asserts a "right," they are essentially brandishing an idea against some more concrete force. Finally, there is the dissatisfying and inadequate measure of law as a response to deadly force. Should we speak of future trials while people are targeted, tortured, and killed? This is further supported by the practical complaint that it is not clear that setting up courts is cheaper, faster, or otherwise more efficient than using more direct methods to physically and immediately halt violence.

Law is also sometimes posited as the bloodless antithesis of political interest or conviction. At its driest, legal formulations can be nearly impenetrable for the layperson, employing technical language and fictitious categorizations. Domestic courts enjoy legitimacy that comes from serving the states in which they operate;[9] this ensures their authority in a manner unavailable to international courts, which must please their state membership bases. For this reason, international courts sometimes resort to exaggerated lawspeak as a means of legitimation. Together with the length of international legal decisions (frequently numbering in the hundreds of pages), this specialist presentation serves to dissuade many curious readers from diving into international criminal jurisprudence, even though nearly all of it is online and freely available (to those with internet access) in just a few clicks.

Leaving law to lawyers is a mistake, however. Regardless of off-putting stylization, legal opinions offer spaces of reasoned dispute. The dispute may be social, political, philosophical, moral, doctrinal; in legal opinions the dispute is rendered (relatively) transparent. Even while we decry the wordy, formalistic, or dry text that too often comprises legal opinion, it is still text. There will be some terms of art that require explication: "stipulation," "summary judgment," even "acquittal" have specific procedural meanings, and a law dictionary, or expertise, can assist for full appreciation. Regardless, a legal opinion drafted by an expert with forty years' experience can be read by an enterprising (and patient) layperson. For many other forms of expertise (economics, quantum mechanics, civil engineering), we cannot say the same. Law hangs in a particular balance, claiming its authority as separate from, yet in service to, the politics of governance. If legal texts are no different from any speech act, then we are all lawyers, and lawyers lose status. But if legal texts grow too esoteric, then the consent of the populace governed—that is, the basis of the Lockean social contract—cannot meaningfully be given.

As regards the delicate balance between expertise and legibility, international criminal law is like domestic law. Decisions produced by international criminal tribunals offer spaces of debate. This debate concerns the definitions of atrocity crimes and, relatedly, the areas of criminality recognized and addressed by international criminal law. It also, importantly, concerns how liability for crimes is attributed. When person X directly commits atrocity Y, the debate space is relatively circumscribed because it looks like the criminal law we know. Modern law builds on hundreds of years of tradition regarding how to attribute responsibility and determine punishment. For atrocity crimes that international criminal law seeks to address, however, we find ourselves in less clearly resolved debates. When armed groups commit atrocity crimes, how do we assess liability for the guys at the top, what the designers of the UN tribunal for Yugoslavia (International Criminal Tribunal for the former Yugoslavia, ICTY) colloquially called the "big fish"? This question is difficult in two respects. First, it is doctrinally difficult: standards are still being developed to assess the criminal responsibility of leaders for the acts of their subordinates, particularly when the order traceable up a clear chain of command is unclear, or where information transmission is spotty. Second, it is politically difficult: in a world where your terrorist is my freedom fighter, assessing the criminality of acts themselves can be a subjective exercise.

The difficulties associated with creating the content of international criminal law doctrine have long provided fodder for theorists.[10] Doctrinal definitions are a standard bugbear for defense counsel, who assert that they preclude the possibility of an effective defense.[11] With the 2018 ICC *Bemba* judgment acquitting the defendant on appeal—discussed in chapter 1—the doctrinal challenges of international criminal law have entered the mainstream of legal practice in direct pronouncement.[12] In *Bemba*, a narrow ICC majority overturned what it characterized as the trial chamber's "strict liability" standard, effectually insisting that the doctrinal challenges underlying international criminal law must be addressed before defendants can be convicted. Similar ideas are on display in the ICC's ongoing investigation of atrocities committed against the Rohingya in Myanmar.[13] The stakes are high and becoming ever more clearly defined.

These doctrinal debates, usually obscured for the layperson by the formal language of court decisions and the structural complexity of institutional design, are formative and crucial and should not be reserved for discussion among international law enthusiasts alone. *The Justice Laboratory* opens some of these debates for inspection, theorizes regarding their consequences, and provides tools for non-jurists to continue exploration on their own.

How to Read This Book

The Justice Laboratory draws from international criminal law, political theory, and sociological methods to help a non-specialist audience understand how international and supranational law seek to constrain state-sponsored violence in Africa.[14] The book visits courts and authorities in Senegal, Chad, Ethiopia, Tanzania, Rwanda, and South Sudan and references The Hague and Geneva. Each of the five chapters takes a different example of legal practice and institutional design and explores aspects of the relevant social, political, and legal impact. Paradigmatic legal problems endemic to the selected institutions are covered and chapters trace how doctrine both creates and reflects institutional and political constraints. The arguments made are based on research from case law, secondary sources, and interviews with actors and observers. Readers may read straight through or jump to chapters of interest: each chapter is a self-contained entity and can be understood in isolation.

Chapter 1 begins with a consideration of the ICC, challenging a mainstream story regarding African "backlash" that suggests African states are particularly backward or corrupt. Instead, African states' appropriation of ICC power and politics showcases a cagey, targeted cooperation with the ICC (and the ICC's acquiescence to the same) that has led to the current crisis for the court. In many parts of Africa where political violence amasses staggering casualties amid breathtaking brutality, international criminal justice mechanisms have been instrumentalized by authoritarian leaders solely to eliminate political opposition, with no discernible learned liberal governance for the countries impacted. The ICC has become a friend to authoritarians seeking to consolidate power in the wake of mass violence, a fact that is masked by the contemporary discussion of African resistance to cooperation with the ICC. For African citizens subject to violence arising from illiberal governance, the quiet and calculated cooperation of African leaders with the ICC has been far more important than their noisy, resistant showboating.

Chapter 1 examines ICC action and reaction structured around two central principles: complementarity and sovereign immunity. The first epoch of ICC work, from its creation through its first self-referral cases, is defined largely by these two concepts. Complementarity is the doctrine that allows the ICC to act only when member states "cannot or will not." It effectively turns the ICC into a court of last resort. Complementarity was a central concept written into the ICC's institutional design in order to quell fears that overzealous prosecutors would abuse their mandate. While the ICC's establishment was an unpredicted achievement, it was followed by another: its docket was quickly filled with a series of self-referral cases from African member states, in what I call the unexpected operationalization of the ICC's complementarity design. Challenging traditional expectations regarding sovereignty,[15] a number of African countries experiencing political violence called on the ICC to help them prosecute atrocity crimes, cooperating extensively with the court to permit its investigators access and handing over arrested suspects. Within a decade of coming into existence, the ICC was busily at work prosecuting African warlords. At present, of the seven African situations the ICC is addressing, five are self-referrals.

While complementarity has provided an institutional victory for the ICC, it has been followed by a pushback against the court by its African member states, often by the very states that requested ICC engagement. This epoch is defined by the question of the possible limitations of sovereign immunity, couched in the language of neocolonialism—that is, a western disrespect or disregard for African systems and leaders. The strength of this pushback should not be underestimated: claims that the ICC "chases" Africans and engages in modern-day colonialism have led the African Union to stage several votes on the question of ordering its member states to withdraw from the court. The *Kenyatta* and *Ruto* cases, as discussed in the chapter, exemplify this challenge. Following electoral violence in Kenya that killed up to 3,000 people in 2007, the ICC Office of the Prosecutor initiated its first independent (that is, not referred by a member state or the UN) investigation.[16] It did so on the request of an independent Kenyan commission, which found that the electoral violence was organized by Kenyan political leaders, and these same leaders were now obstructing its investigation.[17] The leaders of the two opposing parties, Kenyatta and Ruto, successfully parlayed the ICC investigation into political success, working together and winning election after their indictments. The ICC cases against both leaders were eventually dropped after evidence against the defendants evaporated: several witnesses suddenly died, disappeared, or recanted. The contemporary challenge concerns the direction of the ICC as the court tries to move beyond prosecuting the losers to conflicts. The chapter sets out this conflict, showing how the doctrinal rationale behind the ICC's prosecutions is an insufficient answer to the political problems of its practice.

Chapter 2 considers Rwanda, perhaps the world's most concentrated example of the application of international criminal justice. After the world stood by while upward of one million people were slaughtered over a few months' time in 1994, the UN Security Council created an international ad hoc tribunal to try atrocity crimes associated with the genocide. Over two decades, sitting in Tanzania (with an appeals chamber in The Hague), the ICTR heard cases concerning the Rwanda genocide, establishing many facts about its scale and organization. While the ICTR has been critiqued for inefficiency, it has also been celebrated for progressive legal interpretations, particularly as regards sexual violence, an atrocity crime still under-considered by international criminal law.

The story of Rwandan reconciliation—which was the ostensible purpose of the ICTR, beyond its condemnation of several genocidaires—is much more contested. Unlike its sister tribunal for the former Yugoslavia, the ICTR's work was explicitly doctrinally driven by a goal of reconciliation.[18] While Rwandan violence has ended, the question of "reconciliation" is live and unresolved. The Hutu-Tutsi divide that defined the genocide remains intact, reified by a local Tutsi politics that criminalizes discussion of Hutu victims, Hutu saviors, or Tutsi perpetrators. Paul Kagame, the military leader who marched into Kigali in 1994, ended the genocide, and assumed the presidency, has been implicated in massacres of Hutus in Rwanda and Congo, with victims numbering in the hundreds of thousands.[19] He presides over an authoritarian state that brooks no opposition and now rejects cooperation with international criminal tribunals (both the ICTR and the ICC). In August 2017 he stood for a third term and may now rule until 2034.[20] His strongest political rival, Victoire Ingabire, received a fifteen-year jail sentence in 2010 for "minimizing the Rwandan genocide" because she advocates open dialogue that would include Hutu victims. On November 24, 2017, the African Court on Human and Peoples' Rights ruled against Rwanda and ordered it to rehabilitate Ingabire.[21] While Ingabire was released in 2018, prominent members of her party continue to face violence and intimidation; in September 2019 the national coordinator of Ingabire's party was stabbed to death at his workplace by hired assassins.[22] This chapter reviews examples of how international criminal law and its related politics have been put to use in the consolidation of authoritarian power in Rwanda.

In response to what the donor community perceives as the failures of international criminal justice, primarily that it is expensive and enjoys low local buy-in, several hybrid tribunals have been attempted in the past two decades with varying degrees of success. The most recent, and most praised, of these experiments is the Chambres Africaines Extraordinaires (CAE) convened in Dakar, Senegal, to hear the case surrounding Hissène Habré, Chad's deposed ex-president: this court is the subject of chapter 3. Habré fled to Dakar when he fell from power in 1990 and had been living there as a private citizen ever since. Efforts to prosecute Habré gained momentum with the growing popu-

larity of international criminal justice in the 1990s. In 1998, emboldened by
the Pinochet affair, a nongovernmental organization (NGO), Human Rights
Watch, targeted Habré as a good candidate to institute in Africa the norms
and practices of universal jurisdiction—the capacity of any court in any country to hear crimes violating established international criminal law. Yet even
with strong and organized victims' groups operating in Chad, and the singular focus of a global NGO, Habré successfully harnessed Senegalese law and
politics to evade prosecution for nearly two decades. It was only following
a 2012 decision of the International Court of Justice, as well as a change of
leadership in Senegal, that an African Union–organized mechanism was established to try violations committed by Habré and his associates.

The CAE operated on a relatively tiny budget: US$11 million from in-
dictment through appeal. The court maneuvered the delay tactics of Habré's
defense team, stonewalling by Chad, and the unprecedented juridical questions that arose from the hybrid procedure to deliver a judgment and appeal
verdict that caused few political ripples, either inside or outside of Senegal. In
other words, in the contested landscape of international criminal justice, the
CAE was a fulsome success.

The chapter shows how the CAE achieved a wide degree of local legiti-
mization and buy-in in spite of its conviction of an ex-president. The CAE
indicates the potential for local judicial systems to address state-sponsored
atrocity crimes. But because the CAE was only able to convict Habré after he
was out of power, as well as after his political supporters in Senegal were out of
power, the CAE simultaneously highlights an inability for law to speak truth
to those currently enjoying power, a central rule-of-law tenet.

Chapter 4 takes us to the world's newest state, South Sudan, to consider
how international criminal justice addresses oppositional political will. After
achieving independence in 2011, sovereign South Sudan quickly devolved into
brutal violence with casualties said to exceed Syria's. In August 2014, in the
midst of South Sudan's brutal civil war, the African Union released a 315-page
report on South Sudan in which it called, among other things, for a hybrid
tribunal to try violations of international humanitarian law. Emerging from
suggestions offered by civil society organizations regarding how to ensure and
facilitate peace, this tribunal is proposed as a transitional justice mechanism
and is designed to both address the rule of law crisis in the country as well
as set the stage for lasting peace by determining and settling accounts. Both
a tribunal and a truth commission were included in the peace accord signed
between the two warring factions in 2015.

In September 2018 South Sudan's warring factions signed yet another peace accord, with identical provisions for a tribunal and truth commission. The 2018 accord differed from that of 2015 in terms of the number of parties involved and political positions offered: three more years of war only further fractured politics in South Sudan, with an ever-growing number of players insisting that they be paid not to fight. Where the 2015 peace accord was administered by two supranational African organizations, the 2018 treaty was administered by two non-neutral states, Sudan and Uganda, both authoritarian governments with long histories of resisting rule-of-law justice initiatives. The 2019 ouster of Al Bashir in Sudan and ongoing uncertainty regarding leadership in that country have not assisted the process of enforcing the South Sudanese peace accord.

After thirty years of practice, the field of transitional justice is currently undergoing a retrenchment regarding its norms and capacities. This chapter examines the assumptions underlying the proposed tribunal to query how international criminal law, in the form proposed, can address the problems driving violent conflict in South Sudan. Drawing on interviews with actors involved with the development of the proposed hybrid tribunal, the chapter examines the dangers and potential of addressing South Sudanese violence through law.

Chapter 5 brings us to Arusha, Tanzania. Arusha is the location of the ICTR, several regional courts, and Pan-African and regional bar associations, making it a contemporary justice hotspot. African experiments with regional courts have been uneven. The Economic Community of West African States (ECOWAS), serving that part of Africa, would be an example of a successful regional court building a steady body of enforceable jurisprudence; the Southern African Development Community (SADC) tribunal, representing the southern cone and shut down after its first case when it ruled against Zimbabwe, showcases the other extreme. In Arusha there is an interesting emergence of regional jurisprudence challenging state practice from an unexpected source: the East African Court of Justice (EACJ), founded in 2001. This chapter examines the institutional constraints, challenges, and inventions that have enabled the EACJ, nominally a trade court, to take on human rights claims—mostly by prisoners against the Tanzanian government—that elude the African Court of Justice and Human Rights, and how the "justice laboratory" of Arusha, itself, may be contributing to that practice.

The conclusion returns to the book's central question—how supranational judicial institutions might constrain state behavior to protect core rights—and considers two more interesting African interventions: the proposed African Court of Justice and Human Rights, proposed under the Malabo Protocol of

2015, and The Gambia's retooling of the Genocide Convention with its case against Myanmar regarding atrocities committed against the Rohingya. Both of these examples demonstrate how African actors are growing international law in new directions.

From the seventeenth century onward, law has consolidated its place at the center of power in western thought, both as a means to conquer peoples, as well as inoculation against the excesses of leaders. Law is a force that can oppress or enable, build or destroy, make visible or obscure. The examples considered in *The Justice Laboratory* provide new perspectives on the way that international criminal justice has been appropriated by political elites in and in relation to Africa, how this appropriation has led to new legal experiments, and how such experiments operationalize (challenging, applying, and redefining) rule-of-law norms.

ONE

Losing the Battle for Hearts and Minds at the International Criminal Court

In 2015 the staff of the International Criminal Court (ICC), the world's first permanent tribunal with jurisdiction over individuals accused of atrocity crimes, moved into their permanent offices in The Hague. The stunning six-building campus is dominated by a tall glass tower. Inside, a moat separates the hectic, formal security apparatus of metal detectors, bullet-proof glass, and locked revolving gates from the Zen calm of the quiet, light-filled court complex. The Danish architects report that their focus was on the victims. What sort of building would make them feel comfortable? What architecture would communicate the justice mission of the court?

The focus on symbolism is important, because much of the ICC's power resides in its development of norms. Designed as "a court of last resort," representatives of the ICC claim that success will come when the court stands idle. This situation will occur not because of the lack of atrocity crimes, but because states address this criminality themselves. This idea is given juridical form in the ICC's "complementarity jurisdiction" mandate, meaning that the court hears cases only where the states concerned cannot or will not prosecute. This institutional design imagines that states, agreeing with and having internalized the norms and the laws that the ICC represents, will address atrocity crimes committed within their borders, even and especially by their own authorities. This would leave the ICC as a kind of warden or referee in the global system.

Buy-in from states is essential, because the ICC doesn't have a police force or other means of enforcing its edicts. It relies entirely on state cooperation to complete its work. And here, the ICC is in trouble. In 2018, for the first time, the membership roster of state parties decreased, as Burundi renounced its membership; in March 2019 Duerte's Philippines followed suit. As of this writing, 122 countries are members of the ICC, with its strongest contingencies in Europe and Africa. Major world powers, including the United States, Russia, China, and India, have never signed on to the court and are (depending on administration) more or less openly hostile to it.

The greatest existential threat the ICC faces is arguably in Africa, where the entire African membership contingent is in question. African states were early ICC adopters; Senegal was the first state to sign and ratify the Rome Statute, the treaty governing the court, in February 1999. African states figured significantly in the ratification process that constructed the court, providing twenty of the sixty ratifications necessary to establish the court in 2002. The court's singular focus on African crises, together with its two-decade track record of only prosecuting rebels and losing sides in African conflicts, has weakened its brand in Africa, however. Thus, the ICC today has also become synonymous with Pan-African resistance to neocolonial western intervention, where the African Union, supported by many African regimes, encourages states to withdraw from the court. This means that over fewer than twenty years, from the ICC's creation as a global institution created primarily by and for African (and other) states, the ICC has now become one more "western" institution positioned in opposition to Africa, its governments, and its peoples.

There are many possible explanations for how this happened.[1] This chapter tells an institutional story, showing how ICC doctrine was captured by and for local leaders, focusing on two particular legal challenges that characterize ICC practice: complementarity and sovereign immunity. The first section lays out the ideological and historical background that birthed international criminal law as practice and doctrine. The second section examines complementarity and sovereign immunity. Section three dives into cases, focusing on how complementarity has been operationalized into a practice known as "self-referrals" and showing how this has worked badly for the institution. The conclusion summarizes how while some of the blame for how the ICC has fallen from grace in Africa can be handed to a blundering and tone-deaf ICC, most of it actually owes to clever strategic moves made by African leaders. These leaders aligned their interests with the ICC's institutional interests in order to capture the institution to achieve their own ends. This has meant both that an institution designed to reduce government-sponsored atrocities has aligned with and assisted rights-abusing governments and is on the way toward being effectively destroyed by them. If the ICC fails, it will likely be because its promise of neutral judicialization of international crime failed. This will be a grave loss indeed.

"Towards a More Just World": Getting to the ICC

Seeds for the ICC's construction were sown with the Nuremberg tribunal following World War II. Designed by the four victorious European powers, the tribunal was conceptualized even while the war waged. Meeting in Nova Scotia in 1943, when it was clear the Allied powers would win, Stalin, Churchill, and Roosevelt discussed the value of public trials for their enemies. Ironically, one oft-quoted anecdote places Stalin as the rule-of-law brake on a vengeful Churchill. In this telling, when Churchill urged thousands of executions, Stalin countered by suggesting trials. Churchill is said to have replied, "Naturally, we'll try them first!"[2]

The specter of show trials dogged the Nuremberg tribunal (and its successor trials) from the beginning. First, the crimes had to be identified. Of the four crimes tried at Nuremberg, only one of them, "war crimes," can be said to have been recognized under international law before the fact. The other three—crimes against humanity, the waging of aggressive war, conspiracy— were all creative interpretations of existing legal or political ideas. Since law's legitimacy is based in the legality principle, which holds that things must be declared illegal before they are applied to actions (that is, no ex-post-facto law decrees), this was a challenge for the architects of the Nuremberg court.

Next there was the problem of who stood in the dock. At Nuremberg, the four victorious powers tried Germans exclusively, although of course it was not only Germans who committed atrocities in World War II. In order to avoid the most egregious examples of "victor's justice" (which is to say, not justice but rather vengeance), the Allied powers stayed away from charges that would have easily invited a "tu quoque" (literally "you, too") defense. Thus, German firebombing of London was not charged, since the Allied firebombing campaign that obliterated Dresden in 1944, in order to bring Germany to its knees through civilian casualties, was a clear example of a war crime. Casualties from Dresden are estimated at between 25,000 to 35,000 deaths. Likewise, the specter of the Soviet massacre at Katyn in 1941, where more than 20,000 Polish soldiers and officers were executed, required careful constructions of Nazi criminality regarding mass murder when the Soviets were sitting in judgment. Finally, an element of randomness at the Nuremberg tribunal also challenged its rule-of-law status. Lady justice, blindfolded, holds the scales in her hands and weighs the facts. But at Nuremberg, four Allied powers needed to be appeased, not only regarding what was criminalized and what was validated (or at least ignored), but also in terms of who stood in the dock. Each of the Allied powers had invaded and controlled a part of Germany, and each had picked up Nazis in the process. At Nuremberg, there was thus also a political appeasement where each Allied power could give over some of its prisoners to stand trial. This, combined with Hitler's absence, contributed to an unevenness of the trials, where some of the most important and central figures of Hitler's regime, such as Hermann Göring, stood next to relatively unknown figures such as Hans Fritsche, a senior official in Joseph Goebbel's propaganda ministry.

In spite of the flaws outlined above, the Nuremberg trials enjoy a quasi-mythologized status today in western political and legal thought. The trials were presented at the time as the Allied powers' determination to "stay the hand of vengeance"[3] and substitute legal process for violent reprisal. Despite volumes of evidence suggesting that the trials were reprisal in another form, they have entered the cannon as examples of law in place of violence. The Nuremberg trials led to the field of international criminal law, which, in turn, included notions of inviolable, non-derogable human rights vested in individuals, above and beyond their status as citizens of sovereign states.

The Nuremberg tribunals thus helped crystalize a series of ideas that were developed immediately following World War II as a response to the state-sponsored violence of that conflict. Central to these principles is the first right recognized in the 1948 Universal Declaration on Human Rights: the right to life. This right does not disappear because it is not recognized or respected by the state in which the individual happens to live. Moreover, other states affirm that they have an obligation to recognize and protect individuals' rights outside of their own borders. In this way after World War II, international treaties began to challenge a basic tenet of western thought since the 1648 Peace of Westphalia—the absolute sovereignty of states. Following World War II and the Nuremberg trials, the decision by one state to exterminate a portion of its population became other states' business. This was formalized most clearly in the 1948 Genocide Convention and is evident across many international treaties in force today.

Perhaps at this point, the attentive reader is doing the math: between the judgment of the Nuremberg tribunal (1946) and the Rome Statute (1998) and eventual construction of the ICC (2002), there's a sizable time gap. What happened? In short, the Cold War. Alliances forged to beat Hitler fell apart. In the wake of the Nuremberg tribunal, the newly constructed United Nations forged an International Law Commission (ILC) with the aim of defining international crimes and constructing a permanent Nuremberg-style court. The ILC met dutifully, each year, and worked on its definitions. The chasm between the United States and the Union of Soviet Socialist Republics, however, meant that ideas, memos, and discussions were the only tangible fruit of the ILC from 1949 to 1991.

The West "won" the Cold War with the fall of the Berlin Wall and the dissolution of the Soviet state, accomplishing what was at the time hailed as "the end of history."[4] Liberalism was triumphant, and the ILC was ready. ILC materials were put to use on the first western casualty of this new epoch, the violent disintegration of Yugoslavia. In 1993, in the shadow of the first concentration camps in Europe since World War II, the five members of the UN Security Council set up an ad hoc tribunal to hear crimes arising from that conflict. This was to become the International Criminal Tribunal for the former Yugoslavia (ICTY), which in turn became the longest running, most productive international criminal court in history. It was quickly followed in 1994 by the International Criminal Tribunal for Rwanda (ICTR), responding to the Rwanda genocide (the ICTR is discussed in depth in the next chapter). Within four years of the ICTR's creation, states gathered in Rome in 1998 and signed a treaty for an international criminal court. Under the terms of the Rome Statute, after sixty states had signed and ratified it, the ICC would come into being. These signatures and ratifications were accomplished within four years, a lightning-quick process by international standards that surprised and delighted most observers. On July 31, 2002, the ICC began its work as a permanent tribunal sitting in The Hague.

The ICC has subject matter jurisdiction over genocide, crimes against humanity, war crimes, and (since 2018, in practice only for those countries that acquiesce) the crime of aggression. It can only consider those atrocities occurring after July 2002, the date the ICC came into existence. Like all international organizations, it serves its member states who are supposed to guide and manage the court through an Assembly of State Parties (ASP), a body that meets yearly. The ICC can review situations involving individuals from non-member states when such cases are referred by the UN Security Council. This has happened twice, in relation to Libya and Sudan. Otherwise, the ICC hears cases that either its prosecutor independently elects (so far, the only cases to move forward this way concerned Kenya and Côte d'Ivoire, although new investigations have opened in Georgia and Burundi) or those referred by its member states. This last category has constituted the bulk of the ICC's work so far, but with a twist: referrals of situations to the ICC have been self-referrals, in which member states request the court's aid through the ICC's complementarity provisions.

Self-referrals have shown themselves to be the ICC's Trojan Horse: what at first seemed celebratory is in fact the source of destruction. Self-referrals could have been the realization of the norms driving the institution, an actualization of the "buy-in" that is necessary for the ICC to succeed. This would have been a win-win, that is, the ICC doing the work for which it was created in assistance to the member states who created it. This is not how self-referrals have operated, however. Ultimately, they have poisoned the institution, as states have used them politically, to eliminate rivals, for example, but not normatively, to evenly redress state-sponsored violence. This is due to two definitive elements of the ICC's construction that have not functioned as planned, complementarity and sovereign immunity. We consider each in turn.

Doctrinal Innovations:
Complementarity and No Sovereign Immunity

The story of the ICC's development from lofty international lawyerly ideal to metal and glass reality is told definitively by William Schabas, who has, at this writing, produced six editions of his seminal *Introduction to the International Criminal Court*. Schabas provides a lively account of how the international community negotiated this institution, particularly the backroom deals driven by Canada and designed to thwart the hegemony of the United States and the UN Security Council. For my purposes here, I will outline the ICC's design. As noted above, the court emerged from the heady optimism for liberalism's institutions that followed the end of the Cold War, an institution riding the wake of the UN ad hoc tribunals for Yugoslavia and Rwanda. The belief at the time was that these tribunals could use law's rationality to counter barbaric mass violence. Belief is an important word, as there was no empirical evidence (beyond the self-congratulatory legacy of the Nuremberg tribunals, which conveniently overlooks the Tokyo tribunal) to suggest that the foreign policy of international trials was effective at mitigating mass violence or constraining state responsibility for atrocity.[5] The triumph of liberal western democracy in the self-styled conflict between democracy and authoritarianism that had defined the preceding half century provided its own argument for the power of rule-of-law institutions, in which courts are first among equals.

Nonetheless, even if courts were understood to possess near-magic potential to constrain rights-violating politics, there was still concern in the like-minded western liberal powers regarding a too-powerful court overstepping its bounds. Governance theories require a balance of power between the executive, legislative, and judicial where the judiciary applies (but does not create) law. A too-imposing judiciary can represent a threat to democratic governance, since judges are not elected or otherwise representative of an electorate. So, while courts may be magic, they are only good magic when steered by careful, cautious judges keen to apply, not create, law. Again, it is important to recognize this constriction on courts and judges as an ideal type and not a fully realizable policy. Judges apply law, and application requires interpretation, and interpretation is an act of creation.[6] Regardless, rule-of-law practices imagine almost all legal interpretations as predicted by the law as it stands, since future predictability is an essential element of the legality principle. Judges and courts should therefore be conservative, not creative, in their interpretations of law, where conservative means predictable and anticipated. An international court with a global reach could only function as a desired court if it, too, behaved conservatively and in predictable ways.

Here, the careful, plodding practice of the ICTY proved essential in the political will to develop the ICC (the ICTR, discussed in the next chapter, was always a bit more problematic, the Tokyo Tribunal to the ICTY's Nuremberg). The ICTY's first case, against a low-ranking volunteer in a Bosnia-Serb paramilitary group, is demonstrative of this approach. In that case, the ICTY asked and answered, in relentless detail, the questions imagined for studious application of the Geneva Conventions, the treaties that govern the laws of war. That document, from 1949 and expanded in 1977, is built on the distinction between international armed conflict, which it governs in specific detail, and internal armed conflict, about which it only very generally prescribes a basic rights standard. This is a reflection, as discussed above, of the continuing importance of sovereignty: states may decide how they conduct their internal affairs except, following the horrors of World War II, if those affairs threaten the essential human rights of their citizens. In its first judgment (*Tadic*, 1997), the ICTY spent many pages determining what sort of conflict, and therefore what precise elements of law, applied in the case of Yugoslavia's dissolution.[7] This studied, non-activist application of international law standards was central to convincing the like-minded western powers that it was possible to create a reasoned, reasonable global court.

It's good to trust but it's better to secure, and several fail-safes were included in the Rome Statute governing the ICC. The central fight in the ICC's institutional design concerned how it would receive cases—would they be referred by the UN Security Council under its Chapter 7 power under the UN

Charter (this is how the ICTY and ICTR were created), or would the ICC's prosecutor go out and look for them? This latter method corresponds, generally speaking, to how criminal cases come before domestic courts in democracies. The political fight was therefore between how one allocates power and risk: the power and risk of an independent (and possibly rogue) prosecutor capable of scouring the globe for wrongdoing? Or rather the power and risk of further extending the Security Council's reach, effectively enabling a political organ to bring criminal cases against individual actors?

The United States, initially a strong proponent of the ICC, was, of course, in favor of making the ICC essentially an organ of the United Nations and putting responsibility for bringing cases under the ambit of the Security Council. Beyond the obvious self-interest for the United States in maintaining control over the institution, institutional reasons support this solution. The Security Council brings balance (some might say intransigence) to international affairs by giving veto power for any and all UN initiatives to its five permanent members. This system has existed since the UN's founding in 1945, and the five permanent members—the United States, United Kingdom, Russia, China, and France—arguably represent forces in the world that cannot be ignored. Thus, there is some good sense in officially giving the UN Security Council the legal mandate over the court that it already politically enjoys.

Nonetheless, and rather unexpectedly, this is not what happened. Instead, due to the clever maneuverings of a group of states led by Canada, the ICC was constructed not as an organ of the UN, but rather as an independent institution with a prosecutor capable of bringing her or his own cases. This means that the prosecutor, acting on his or her own initiative (what are called *propio motu* powers), determines what situations in the world merit the court's attention.

Naturally, checks and balances exist. First, the prosecutor must seek the approval of a pre-trial chamber of ICC judges in order to formally commence an investigation into a situation, the necessary forerunner of bringing charges against a defendant. An example of how this can act as a check on the prosecutor: in April 2019 a pre-trial chamber at the ICC stopped the prosecutor's investigation of crimes committed in Afghanistan (although this was reversed on appeal and the investigation may now go ahead).[8] This investigation threatens to catch U.S. military personnel and is consequently vigorously opposed by the American administration. Political unpopularity should not, normally, be a recognized reason not to bring a case. In the Afghanistan case the pre-trial chamber characterized the anticipated U.S. resistance to a proposed ICC investigation as a rationale that spoke against ICC inquiry. This baseline realism was euphemistically labeled the "interests of justice" by the pre-trial chamber, a turn of phrase that evoked ire followed by soul searching in the international criminal law community.[9]

Second, admissibility before the court imagines that a case must meet a "gravity" threshold, which is a category imagined by the Rome Statute itself in Article 17(1)(d). Gravity was the issue at stake in Israel's interference with a vessel registered to an ICC member state in conjunction with the blockade of Gaza in 2010.[10] Israel is not a member of the ICC, but some of its policies toward Palestinians arguably constitute atrocity crimes within the court's jurisdiction. Given the highly politicized geopolitical situation of Israel and its treatment of Palestinians, the case was a political tinderbox for the ICC. Although the ICC quenched this spark by finding the "gravity" threshold was not met in the case,[11] the Office of the Prosecutor (OTP) has recently opened another investigation relating to events since June 13, 2014.

Finally, the UN Security Chamber has two methods by which it can intervene directly. Under Rome Statute Article 16, it can request a one-year deferral of investigation and can do so an unlimited number of times. This failsafe, introduced to protect in situations where peace processes might be threatened by judicial investigations or other political interests, has never been invoked. As noted above, the UN Security Council can also, inversely, refer situations to the ICC and, in this way, ask the prosecutor to investigate situations that the ICC otherwise might not be permitted to investigate, as nominally the ICC is a membership-based court. This has occurred in two cases: Libya and Sudan. Neither case has been a success for the ICC and will be discussed further below.

Complementarity

The formalities of jurisdiction listed above constitute a series of checks on the power of the prosecutor and the institution vis à vis its member states. Yet complementarity is arguably the most substantial check on the ICC's reach. Complementarity is what makes the ICC a "court of last resort." It relates to the admissibility of cases before the court. Jurisdiction concerns areas in which the court is competent to decide cases. Admissibility relates to whether cases in the court's area actually come to the court. Complementarity holds that cases admissible before the court are only those cases in which "the State is unwilling or unable genuinely to carry out the investigation or prosecution."[12]

In a word, complementarity ensures that states always get a first crack at adjudicating criminality on their terrain or involving their citizens. Complementarity is thus a safeguard for sovereignty because articulating criminality and punishing it is a central state function. Max Weber famously defined statehood as a monopoly on the legitimate use of violence. Granting outside actors control over legitimate violence (where the trial and imprisonment of people is understood as violence) directly implicates state sovereignty, striking at the heart of what a state is. Complementarity protects sovereignty even while giving it away—to a supranational organization granted a role in applying state violence—by making states first in the adjudication of atrocity crimes. The ICC prioritizes states by granting itself jurisdiction only where states cannot or will not adjudicate.

It is important to underscore that complementarity is not intended to permit the ICC an oversight role over cases' eventual resolution; the ICC is not supposed to "check states' work" and intervene when dissatisfied. In this way, complementarity creates an international criminal justice organization that nevertheless puts states first. It is this that led the first ICC prosecutor, Luis Moreno-Ocampo, to declare that a successful ICC will be a dormant ICC, where states are prosecuting their own criminal actors.[13]

Complementarity was the jewel of the ICC when the Rome Statute was drafted. To be sure, at the time there were arguments against complementarity and in favor of a more powerful, invasive court. This is because supranational courts add value by enforcing norms that are difficult to put into place domestically. Consider the European Court of Human Rights (ECHR), the most successful and active human rights court in history. That court, which serves forty-seven member states, hears cases brought by citizens against their own states. When the ECHR rules against a state, that state must change its practice, enact legislation, or undertake other actions to bring itself into conformity with the European Convention on Human Rights, the document guiding the ECHR's decisions. The ECHR has no police power yet still claims a near perfect compliance rate.[14] This compliance arises from states choosing to bind themselves to a supranational authority. The reasons why states would do so are numerous and include strengthening their reputation as human rights protectors as well as pushing back against populism or other rights-challenging aspects of majority rule.[15]

The ECHR requires that citizens exhaust domestic remedies before bringing a case before it. This therefore positions the ECHR as the final arbiter of rights claims against states in the territories it serves. In international law practice, it is common to structure courts in a position that grants them a final say. Both the ICTY and ICTR were the top and final authorities regarding atrocity crimes committed in Bosnia and Rwanda, although this control depended upon these countries existing as international protectorates. Complementarity, by contrast, imagines states as the top and final authorities as regards atrocity crimes committed on their territory or by their citizens. States are the first and, so long as they act, last actors. Provided states can and do act, complementarity recognizes states themselves as the final arbiters of criminality within their borders or committed by their citizens.

Now because we are talking about law, there is flexibility of interpretation regarding what "cannot or will not" entail, and since it is the ICC making the determination, the power of interpretation (and thereby a form of final arbitration) lies with it.[16] In the same article discussing admissibility (that is, the ICC's complementarity jurisdiction), the Rome Statute clarifies that "unwillingness" on the part of the state can be shown through court proceedings undertaken "for the purpose of shielding the person concerned from criminal responsibility"; where there has been "unjustified delay in the proceedings which in the circumstances is inconsistent with an intent to bring the person concerned to justice"; or there is a problem concerning the "independent" or "impartial" conduct of the proceedings. We can see the potential for ICC interpretation in each of these clauses.[17]

Complementarity is at the center of the ICC's political problem in Africa, but it is not complementarity as it was imagined by the drafters of the Rome Statute, that is, the state-empowering doctrine situating the ICC as secondary to states. Rather, complementarity has been harnessed by a number of African states through self-referrals to the ICC. Member states can refer situations in other member states to the ICC; recall that this is one of the ways that the court can take a case, the other two being the prosecutor exercising her *propio motu* powers and referral from the UN Security Council. Yet no African member state has referred another to the ICC, to date; as of this writing, the sole instance of state referral by another state is the 2018 referral of Venezuela by six South American states, an unprecedented and juridically exciting event. Outside this recent development, the history of referral situations at the ICC is member states referring themselves, under complementarity, by asserting that they do not have the resources to try the individuals concerned. All of the convictions rendered by the ICC to date are self-referrals. The details of how this practice has functioned toxically for the ICC are considered below. Before moving to this discussion, however, it is necessary to visit another doctrinal element of ICC innovative practice: its rejection of sovereign immunity.

Sovereign Immunity

Sovereign immunity is the practice of protecting individuals acting on behalf of the state from prosecution. It is a political protection that makes statecraft possible by ensuring that representatives of the state are free to act on behalf of the state without fear of extrajudicial meddling. States cannot conduct necessary state business if their representatives are not free to travel the globe without fear of arrest, and sovereign immunity is the legal concept that assures this political necessity.

International criminal law conflicts directly with established notions of sovereign immunity. This is because it takes as its subject matter acts of state determined to be beyond the pale of what is protected as statecraft. The crimes recognized under international criminal law—genocide, crimes against humanity, and war crimes—are understood to fall outside of accepted political behavior. These crimes involve the violation of rights held to be inalienable and non-derogable, meaning that no compelling circumstances can be named to contextualize, excuse, or mitigate the criminality of the acts recognized as illegal under international criminal law. What this means in terms of sovereign immunity is that state representatives engaging in acts that violate international criminal law do not enjoy immunity, because these are not legitimate acts of state. The ICC does not recognize any privilege for state representatives in its practice.

The contemporary standard bearer that showcases the difficulties of finding a balance between protecting the legal fiction that allows states to agitate in the world through their human representatives and that would nonetheless constrain the atrocity crimes committed by or on behalf of states by human representatives is found in the 2002 case between the Democratic Republic of the Congo and Belgium before the International Court of Justice (ICJ), known by students of international law as the *Arrest Warrant Case*.[18] Congo brought the case against Belgium, because the latter arrested Abdulaye Yerodia Ndombasi for atrocity crimes committed while he was Congo's foreign minister. The ICJ ruled that Yerodia enjoyed immunity from prosecution before Belgian courts regardless of the charges against him for reasons of sovereign immunity; although Yerodia was sought by Belgium in relation to atrocity crimes, the ICJ ruled that Yerodia's government position rendered him untouchable by the Belgian court.

This decision, produced by the granddaddy of international courts pronouncing on international law, might have effectively spelled the end of international criminal law. Recall that international criminal law is constructed on the precept that certain criminal acts must be considered outside the realm of permissible statecraft. No matter how beneficial to a political cause or platform crimes against humanity, war crimes, or genocide may be, they are non-derogable, that is, non-mitigable by context, and wholly impermissible. Finding that sovereign immunity shields individuals from considerations of atrocity crimes would effectively end the field of international criminal law.

The *Arrest Warrant Case* judgment included two critical, though conceptually incoherent, paragraphs saving the enterprise, however. First, the ICJ specified that immunity does not mean impunity:

> The Court emphasizes, however, that the immunity from jurisdiction enjoyed by incumbent Ministers for Foreign Affairs does not mean that they enjoy impunity in respect of any crimes they might have committed, irrespective of their gravity. Immunity from criminal jurisdiction and individual criminal responsibility are quite separate concepts. While jurisdictional immunity is procedural in nature, criminal responsibility is a question of substantive law. Jurisdictional immunity may well bar prosecution for a certain period or for certain offences; it cannot exonerate the person to whom it applies from all criminal responsibility.[19]

Although this doesn't provide much practical guidance regarding how, precisely, suits might precede, it is still an important distinction, recognizing that acting on behalf of the state does not offer umbrella protections for consideration of the criminality of actions.

Second, the ICJ laid out four conditions wherein prosecution would still be possible. The first three effectively covered prosecution by the state itself (that is, situations not involving sovereign immunity on the international stage between sovereign states). The ICJ then added:

> Fourthly, an incumbent or former Minister for Foreign Affairs may be subject to criminal proceedings before certain international criminal courts, where they have jurisdiction. Examples include the International Criminal Tribunal for the former Yugoslavia, and the International Criminal Tribunal for Rwanda, established pursuant to Security Council resolutions under Chapter VI1 of the United Nations Charter, and the future International Criminal Court created by the 1998 Rome Convention. The latter's Statute expressly provides, in Article 27, paragraph 2, that "[i]mmunities or special procedural rules which may attach to the official capacity of a person, whether under national or international law, shall not bar the Court from exercising its jurisdiction over such a person."

With this paragraph, the ICJ carved out an exception for certain international tribunals, a sort of technical workaround for the overriding rule of sovereign immunity.

What this effectively means is that sovereign immunity is simultaneously protected and not protected. In the ICJ decision, the thumbs up or down to sovereign immunity rests entirely on the specificity of where it's being applied. The ICJ rejected the capacity for a Belgian national court, applying universal jurisdiction over atrocity crimes, to issue an international arrest warrant for a Congolese official on trial for acts that occurred while he was a state representative. Universal jurisdiction, which is discussed further in chapter 3 regarding Senegal's trial of Hissène Habré, enables national courts to try those crimes for which there is universal concurrence that they cannot be legal. This in turn is a central part of what legitimizes international criminal law itself, particularly what allows international criminal law to keep growing its jurisprudence forward, in a "progressive" way, often before the notions articulated in that jurisprudence have been written down (that is, the types of violations of the legality principle that we saw in the Nuremberg tribunals). Thus, the ICJ *Arrest Warrant Case* allows a middle ground where international criminal tribunals like the ICC and ICTR are legitimized and protected. Other tribunals, like the CAE in Senegal, discussed in chapter 3, or the proposed Hybrid Court for South Sudan (HCSS), discussed in chapter 4, and the expansive and creative East African Court of Justice (EACJ), discussed in chapter 5, might fall outside this recognized protection. This means that the institutional structure of international criminal law, where certain tribunals are recognized as having jurisdiction over atrocity crimes and in fact exist because of it, survives the ICJ ruling. It also means that other applications of the ideas on which international criminal law is built—centrally the notion that atrocity crimes are not legitimate acts of state and that this universal recognition is legitimately the subject of national jurisdictions—are not accepted by the ICJ. This is the incoherence of the decision: if you do not have a legitimate legal ideal (atrocity crimes not constituting defensible statecraft), then it is hard, ultimately, to accept that any international institution should have jurisdiction over such acts.

So as regards the law, sovereign immunity is left in a somewhat muddled state following the ICJ's *Arrest Warrant Case*, where the case-length discussion of the concept related an incoherent policy rationale. As regards politics, sovereign immunity in Africa has proven to be a powder keg for the ICC. There are many theories regarding why the ideology of sovereign authority is so persistent and popular across the continent. For the sovereign, or head of state, it's great, sure. But what about absolute sovereignty is good for all the non-sovereigns who have to live under him (and it is, nearly always, a him)? Mahmood Mamdani, a giant in African studies and social theory, argues that the nineteenth-century scramble for Africa by European nations set on draining African resources, with consequences still impacting most Africans' daily lives, might provide one explanation; the nearness of this history might make sovereign control all the more precious.[20] There are also theories of patriarchy and cultural identity, where a strong sovereign is a point of pride for those who identify with him.[21] Or perhaps it is nothing more complicated than no sovereign enjoys limiting power, and where one can avoid it, one does.

Politically, the question of immunity for sovereigns, including for atrocity crimes, has proven to be a bit do-or-die across Africa. It led to the near exit of South Africa, originally one of the ICC's strongest proponents and a key rule-of-law ally in Africa, from the court over the incident regarding South Africa's failure to arrest Sudan's Al Bashir when he was still in power and visited that country.[22] It has also prompted an explicit no-sovereign-trials clause in the African Union's proposal for an African criminal court, which is discussed further in the conclusion. It underwrites the African Union's campaign to pressure all its member states to leave the ICC, an event that, were it to happen, would devastate the court.[23]

This makes the ICC's approach to sovereign immunity, reiterated recently in yet another consideration of the non-arrest of Sudan's Omar Al-Bashir, this time by Jordan, all the more unfortunate.[24] The problem of sovereign immunity has arisen again and again in ICC jurisprudence in relation to the now former leader of Sudan. What is doubly unfortunate is that this self-inflicted legal muddle has resulted from what is essentially a political problem. The warrant for Al-Bashir's arrest arose from investigations the ICC prosecutor conducted at the behest of the United Nations. The situation in Sudan is one of only two situations referred to the court by the UN Security Council under its Chapter 7 power, in conjunction with Article 13(b) of the Rome Statute. Neither Sudan nor Libya (the other situation referred by the UN Security Council) are members of the ICC, and investigation of atrocity crimes by the prosecutor in those countries is only made possible through UN Security Council referral. Referral of non-members, however, presumes domestic resistance to ICC investigation, since countries that are willing to permit the ICC to investigate atrocity crimes within their borders or undertaken by their citizens are presumably members of the court. The UN did not provide such assistance, however, beyond the original referral. Thus, the ICC has had to lean on its member states to do the work that the UN Security Council has not done, and in this way, a political challenge has been transformed into a legal challenge.

The latest legal expression on this subject is a bit of a disaster for the court. In May 2019 the Appeals Chamber issued a ruling against Jordan for its non-arrest of Al-Bashir when he visited that country on official business in 2017. Five appeals judges issued four separate opinions, some concurring in part and some dissenting in part. This hodgepodge of legal thought is already non-ideal, as court watchers have noted.[25] More problematic, however, was the manner in which the court glossed over the legal question of what an absence of sovereign immunity before it, which is relatively non-controversial jurisdictionally, might mean in terms of how third-party states should act. The ICC's arrest warrant against Al-Bashir requires third countries, if they are ICC member states, to arrest Al-Bashir should he enter their territory. The ICC has brought cases against South Africa, Jordan, Uganda, and Djibouti for not fulfilling their member-state duties. By one count, thirty-three countries ignored the ICC's arrest warrant against Al-Bashir.[26] But as we see in the discussion regarding sovereign immunity above, including the ruling by the ICJ, sovereign immunity is constructed precisely to protect the capacity of states to do business with other states by shielding their physical (human) representatives from criminal prosecution or other forms of interference. Thus, states stand in very different relation to other states' sovereigns as compared with international courts. This is essentially the conclusion of the ICJ in the *Arrest Warrant Case*; Belgian courts may not criminally prosecute Congo's representative for crimes that have no recognizable statecraft content. States are distinct from international organizations, even if they are applying the same laws, norms, or principles. States may not act against other state representatives, under the doctrine of sovereign immunity, even when certain international organizations can.

When a leading professor of international law raised this point on a popular international law blog,[27] none other than the ICC spokesperson responded, snarkily chiding him for not sufficiently reading, or perhaps not understanding, the judgment. This unleashed a torrent of rebuke as other specialists weighed in to critique the judgment, the institution, and the spokesperson who appeared to be seeking to silence debate and the critique. These clumsy steps by the ICC are all the more problematic for being taken within the community that comprises the ICC's strongest allies, that is, law professors and international law practitioners.

If the ICC's sovereign immunity jurisprudence and discussion has proved clumsy, it is a blunt clumsiness that often accompanies international decisions.

It is the ICC's complementarity jurisprudence that has most endangered the court. The next section looks at how complementarity, which was designed to strengthen the court and create an allyship between it and its member states, has actually weakened the court. This is a story of political savvy on the part of African leaders and political blindness on the part of the ICC. The story emerges from the cases, and they are reviewed below.

ICC Complementarity Practice in Africa

As of this writing, thirty-seven individuals have been charged with atrocity crimes by the ICC, and all of them come from Africa.[28] Of those charges, four individuals have been convicted: Lubanga, Katanga, Al-Mahdi, and Ntaganda. All four of these cases arise from self-referrals, that is, all the convicted defendants were at odds with the prevailing regimes in the countries that referred them to the ICC. Another four individuals, again all self-referrals, have been acquitted: Ngudjolo, Bemba, Gbagbo, and Blé Goudé. Finally, three cases, all *propio motu* cases pursued by the prosecutor, have collapsed before trial.

What makes a court a "good," "legitimate," and "effective" court? The answer cannot simply be its conviction rate. A court that only convicts is not likely to be understood as a rule-of-law institution. At the same time, a court that acquits a great deal also seems to signal a problematic institution. While acquittals are sometimes celebrated as evidence of courts' professionalism and objectivity, they can also represent a significant misuse of resources, both by the institution bringing an ultimately failed prosecution, as well as by the defendant, caught up in the state's machinery. Collapsed cases, on the other hand, are neither celebratable as convictions nor defensible as necessary components of a court's professionalism and objectivity: collapsed cases indicate error and failure, and, as we shall discuss below, the fact that the ICC prosecutor independently brought cases that have failed is significant for the institution.

There are many measurements that determine courts' legitimacy or authority, including the speed of adjudication, the availability of resources to judges and parties, the transparency of ways of working, and final determinations. For the discussion below, as we consider the work of the ICC, we will focus on the most normatively important: predictability and generalizability.

Predictability speaks to the legality principle: cases are brought based on established law, and this law provides guidance as to their likely outcomes. This does not mean that we know precisely what the outcome will be—if this were so, judges and lawyers could be replaced by machines. Rather, it speaks to the legibility of the outcome: does the outcome comport with what we understand of law? International law theorist Martti Koskenniemi (2005) compares this sort of exercise to grammar, which doesn't tell you what to say in a sentence, but instantly conveys when you've constructed a sentence incorrectly.

Generalizability is related to predictability in that it, too, shares a basis in the legality principle. But here we would add notions of non-discrimination and constitutionalized protections for defendants. We do not convict someone because she is a fascist, a Nazi, or an underaged soldier; we convict based on criminal acts, and identify elements that help contextualize these acts, perhaps impacting what crimes we charge or punishments we exact. International criminal law cases should not be so context specific that they do not articulate generalizable principles or conclusions. Where international criminal law judgments indicate unpredictable applications of doctrine or produce non-generalizable conclusions, we should question their value as good, effective, or legitimate.

The sections that follow examine three categories of ICC case outcomes. As noted, most ICC cases are self-referrals, and here predictability and generalizability are implicated because the defendants find themselves before the ICC primarily because of their identity (that is, as individuals on losing political sides). The first two cases considered showcase this dynamic. The first section looks at the ICC's first conviction, against Thomas Lubanga (2012), where the prosecutor ultimately proved no more than what the defendant had freely admitted: children were part of his armed forces. The second section examines the case against Jean-Pierre Bemba, another self-referral. Bemba was arrested in Belgium on his way back to the Democratic Republic of the Congo (DRC) from the United States. He believed he was immune from prosecution because he hadn't committed crimes personally and because he was essential to the peace process. Bemba's eventual acquittal in 2018 demonstrates another challenge to rule-of-law predictability and generalizability, situated in the amorphous contours of international criminal law doctrine. Finally, the third section examines the ICC's "black eyes," its collapsed cases against Kenyan politicians and the acquittal of Côte d'Ivoirian politicians based on the prosecutor's inability to "make a case to answer."[29] Here we see how local political will supersedes the ICC's powers.

The Failure of Self-Referrals:
Lubanga and Ituri, Democratic Republic of the Congo

Crimes committed in Ituri, the mineral rich region of the Democratic Republic of the Congo that borders Rwanda and Uganda, are the subjects of the first "situation" investigated by the ICC prosecutor.[30] The violence in DRC belies comprehension. It has been called "the rape capital of the world" and "the worst place on earth to be a woman." In 2018 Dr. Denis Mukwege Mukengere was awarded the Nobel Peace Prize for his work treating young girls and women who are victims of crippling sexual assault in eastern DRC. The number of victims, as well as the prevalence of such crimes against even very small children, is staggering. From 1998 to 2004, approximately six million people are believed to have died violently in DRC, making it the second deadliest global conflict after World War II.[31] This violence has not ended. As this manuscript was being finalized, the second largest Ebola outbreak in history was taking place in eastern DRC, with the rising death toll blamed on the ongoing violence in remote areas making response and treatment difficult. In August 2021 the UN raised an alarm over "mass rapes" occurring in a southeastern DRC province, where hundreds of rapes perpetrated by armed groups were reported across twelve villages in the span of a few weeks.[32]

Violence in Congo is related to conflicts over resource extraction and the control of profits. The conflict that broke out in 1998 was called "Africa's Seven Nation War" and may in fact have engaged up to twelve countries.[33] Thomas Lubanga, the first defendant charged and convicted by the ICC,[34] led a paramilitary group active in Ituri that opposed the DRC regime and was backed by (and some said controlled by) Rwanda and Uganda. Captured by the Kabila regime, Lubanga was handed over to the ICC when Kabila "invited" the ICC to prosecute him: this was the ICC's first self-referral. In the ensuing years, all prosecutions regarding the DRC have related to Kabila's opponents, including the man who would oppose him for the presidency, Jean-Pierre Bemba.[35]

The *Lubanga* case is a case study in mismanagement and mistake; it was also the ICC's first case, so growing pains are to be expected. The case took six years from arrest to judgment, a length of time that challenges human rights obligations for a speedy trial. Two years into the investigation, mismanagement by the prosecutor resulted in the pre-trial chamber suspending the case, although it eventually moved forward. Extensive problems related to the collection of witness statements by self-interested intermediaries employed by the ICC resulted in the court rejecting and throwing out all the witness statements as biased.[36] The conviction in 2012 found Lubanga guilty of enlisting child soldiers, a fact that he had never contested but rather stipulated to throughout the trial. (Lubanga maintained that he was aware that he had children in his armies, that he sought repeatedly to discharge them, but that he could not keep them out.) The systemic violence plaguing the Ituri region—children abducted from villages and forced into military and sexual service—was not adjudicated in the *Lubanga* case. The eventual sentence of fourteen years in jail was both unreasonably harsh (considering that the OTP did not prove any crime beyond that which Lubanga had admitted, that is, that children under the age of sixteen were present in his army) and infuriatingly lenient, given the horror of violence in Ituri.

In DRC-related cases that have followed *Lubanga*, the ICC has not done much to address the flaws of its experience in this case. Convictions against Katanga (2014) and Ntaganda (2019) have not addressed the extensive violence committed by paramilitary groups in Ituri. These cases thus arguably misrepresent, and possibly even ignore, the most serious crimes committed there. Many observers qualify these defendants as "small fish," that is, not the important government leaders that the ICC should be prosecuting. Like the *Ongwen* case against a former child soldier accused of committing atrocities in Uganda, these cases underline how the ICC avoids prosecuting regime leaders and, instead, focuses on crimes committed by opponents of the regime. Another way to state the problem is to note, as Mark Kersten does, that the ICC has not opened a single case against a state leader since 2011, and that the court risks becoming an institution that "only prosecutes rebels."[37]

The Failure of Doctrine: Bemba *and the Return to Process*

In 2018 a legal bombshell exploded: Jean-Pierre Bemba, convicted by the ICC Trial Chamber in 2016, was acquitted by the Appeals Chamber by a three to two majority ruling.[38] This determination astounded observers and sent shock waves throughout the international criminal law community. Jean-Pierre Bemba was a presidential candidate in DRC in 2006, part of the opposition to Kabila discussed above in relation to the ICC's first conviction, *Lubanga*. Bemba came before the ICC in a self-referral from the Central African Republic (CAR), where he was leading troops opposing the Kabila regime in DRC.

In 2016 Bemba was sentenced to eighteen years in prison for his role, as military commander, for atrocities committed in CAR. The 2016 conviction was significant because it assigned criminal responsibility to a senior military official physically removed from the violence and because it made sexual violence a centerpiece of the charges. Sexual violence, a staple of war, has long been absent from international criminal law's charge sheets. By assigning Bemba responsibility for the rapes committed by fighters under his command, the 2016 trial court judgment was seen as an important doctrinal advance for international criminal law. Thus, the 2018 acquittal was a hard blow for proponents of recognition of sexual violence in international criminal law.

I consider the *Bemba* acquittal not as regards sexual violence charges, but rather as regards how international criminal law tackles questions of process and defendants' rights. In acquitting Bemba, the Appeals Chamber made three novel judicial interpretations. First, the *Bemba* majority found that the ICC prosecution did not sufficiently specify the charges against the defendant. International criminal courts have traditionally employed relatively lenient standards of precision in pre-trial indictments and charge sheets and permitted the prosecutor relatively wide latitude in amending the charges, including during trial. The Appeals Chamber, however, found that simply alerting Bemba to the *categories* of charges he faced (rape, murder, pillage) was not sufficient to later bring precise instances not named prior to trial.[39]

Second, the *Bemba* majority addressed the question of the appropriate standard of review for appellate bodies. Appellate courts rule on questions of how the law is interpreted and applied, turning to questions of fact only when such facts cannot, as a matter of law, stand as interpreted by the trial court. Thus, the typical appellate chamber defers to the trial chamber as regards findings of fact. The *Bemba* majority, however, held "when the Appeals Chamber is able to identify findings [of fact] that can reasonably be called into doubt, it must overturn them."[40] This would seem to invite appeals courts to relitigate cases heard by trial courts. Anticipating this objection, the Appeals Chamber emphasized, "This is not a matter of the Appeals Chamber substituting its own factual findings for those of the trial chamber. It is merely an application of the standard of proof [beyond a reasonable doubt.]"[41] Importantly, even while acquitting Bemba, the Appeals Chamber found him guilty of witness tampering. Given that the witness tampering for which Bemba and some of his cohorts were convicted arguably had a direct impact on some of the testimony that the Appeals Chamber found to be "in doubt," the Appeals Chamber decision could be construed as directly rewarding Bemba's witness interference. The Appeals Chamber judgment made no mention of how Bemba's conviction for obstruction of justice might have altered the evidence it was assessing.

Finally, applying its interpretation of appropriate appellate review, the Appeals Chamber majority reconsidered Bemba's conviction under the doctrine of command responsibility. Command responsibility is the doctrine that attributes criminal liability to leaders based on the crimes committed by their subordinates. Three out of five Appeals Chamber judges found that the Trial Chamber improperly determined that Bemba did not take "all necessary and reasonable" measures when it convicted him. Specifically, the majority challenged what it found were unsubstantiated interpretations regarding Bemba's intent. The Trial Chamber applied a standard that amounted to asking what it was that Bemba *should have done* not to break the law. The Appeals Chamber took issue with this, as well as the fact that Bemba was never informed of this standard.

The 2018 *Bemba* appeals judgment arguably signals a change in direction for the ICC. Other cases have recognized evidentiary ambiguities and inconsistencies. The three cases of *Kenyatta, Ruto,* and *Gbagbo and Blé Goudé,* discussed below, were dismissed when evidence dissolved (witnesses changed their stories, disappeared, or died, some by murder). In the ICC's first judgment, *Lubanga,* all witness testimony was ultimately found to have been tainted and was thrown out by the Trial Chamber. Yet *Bemba* is the first case where, after years of effort, evidentiary inconsistencies resulted in acquittal. More significant, the *Bemba* majority's language, arguing against international criminal law as a form of "strict liability,"[42] signals the possibility of a changing direction in terms of how legal doctrine is applied and interpreted. To the degree that international criminal law has evolved into a field where the strongest defense is "rupture" of the proceedings themselves,[43] this new direction has great positive potential.

Rights advocates and victims lament that substantive justice is not served when defendants are acquitted on procedural grounds. Here the language of ICC judges Christine van den Wyngaert and Howard Morrison in their concurrence in the judgment is instructive. They note that while acquittal on a procedural technicality is "regrettable" for victims, it nonetheless constitutes "the price that must be paid in order to uphold fundamental principles of fairness and the integrity of the judicial process."[44] With its narrow majority and its bombshell reception, however, it is not clear this new focus on procedural legitimacy will hold.

There is much to celebrate in a renewed procedural vigor that prioritizes defendants' rights within the ICC chambers; after all, you cannot hold a trial if you're not prepared to apply procedural safeguards vigorously. Bear in mind that not all post-conflict social transformation need be by trial: lustration and other limitations on government (such as administrative penalties for membership in proscribed groups) can signal a change between past power practices and the present. If one wants to put individuals on trial, however, there must be procedural protections. One such protection is a clear specification of the crime charged and the proof in hand.

Of course, procedural standards at international criminal law may be drawn differently than they would be at domestic law. War zones are difficult places for fact collection, and it seems problematic to allow the very violence that defendants participate in to guarantee that they cannot be prosecuted, because evidence is impossible to safely collect in a timely and reliable manner.

Charges related to sexual violence are particularly fraught in this regard. Sexual violence, although pervasive in war, has faced slow doctrinal development under international criminal law. Victims of sexual violence are often slow to come forward, or slow to report sex crimes as part of the litany of what they have suffered. In addition to being very personal (and thus inappropriate to discuss with strangers taking a witness statement), in many communities, sexual violence carries deep and pervasive stigma against victims. The 2016 *Bemba* judgment was seen as an important victory for substantive justice as regards sexual violence in war, an important step in carrying us toward the "more just world" the ICC celebrates.

Heightened scrutiny for evidentiary matters is arguably a challenge to future prosecutions for sexual violence. At the same time, the *Bemba* trial court judgment's focus on sex crimes and its doctrinal findings regarding how sexual violence is articulated through international humanitarian law were significant, and these doctrinal connections stand, unimpacted by the acquittal since it did not address them.

The Failure of Politics: Kenyatta, Ruto, *and* Gbagbo-Blé Goudé *Cases*

Finally, we turn to the ICC's bêtes noires—instances where the prosecution's cases fell apart, leaving defendants either free, pending further evidence, or acquitted entirely. The greatest ICC failure in this regard concerns the 2011 summons of Uhuru Muigai Kenyatta and William Samoei Ruto. The slow-motion dissolution of the ICC's cases against these two defendants corresponds to the ICC's changed fortunes, from up-and-coming international justice organization to an institution increasingly close to pariah status.

The situation in Kenya, from which the cases against Kenyatta and Ruto emerged, was the ICC's first self-generated investigation, that is, a case the Office of the Prosecutor initiated itself. Following contested elections in 2007 in Kenya, more than 1,000 people were killed in ethnically targeted violence. A government commission known as the Waki Commission (after its chairperson) was set up to investigate the violence. It found that police were responsible for hundreds of murders,[45] and that the government had failed to take the necessary actions to quell the violence. It identified several individuals responsible for incitement to violence in ethnic communities and called on the government to set up a special tribunal to adjudicate the crimes committed within forty-five days of the issuance of its report, after which it promised to send its findings on to the ICC. The Kenyan government did not react and the Waki Commission acted as it promised, sending its materials on to the ICC. Kenya is a member state of the ICC, and this seemed a textbook case for complementarity, using the court where a state could not or would not address the situation on its own. The situation in Kenya became the prosecutor's first *propio motu* investigation.

On its face, the situation in Kenya appeared to speak directly to the ICC's raison d'être: a member state, suffering political violence that its institutions could recognize but did not have sufficient clout to press forward with a case, was seeking supranational assistance. Enter the ICC, adding value in response to the member state's request for help (articulated not by the regime but by a state institution created for the purpose). This investigation of Kenya fit the bill precisely for the ICC as court of last resort. Yet the situation in Kenya played out exactly the opposite: the ICC's investigation of political violence actually helped propel the defendants it was investigating to power and created an existential threat to the court by igniting the African "pushback" that has defined discussion of the court's work in Africa ever since.

Kenyatta and Ruto were influential supporters of opposition parties named by the Waki Commission to have been instrumental in inciting the postelection violence. In 2010 the ICC summoned Kenyatta to appear, and in 2011 it expanded its summons to include Ruto and others. The Kenyan government challenged the ICC's jurisdiction on admissibility grounds, and the defendants, while protesting their innocence, made scheduled appearances before the court via video-link. In 2012 the pre-trial chamber confirmed the defendants' indirect co-perpetration of crimes against humanity including murder, forced displacement, rape, persecution, and other inhumane acts.[46] The trial was set to begin in 2013.

In the meantime, one-time adversaries Uhuru Kenyatta and William Ruto came to power in Kenya following March 2013 elections and the victory of their four-party coalition. Their campaign built on the indictments issued by the ICC, making political hay from what they called neocolonial meddling from waning imperialist powers. Kenyatta assumed the presidency and Ruto the vice presidency. While continuing to pledge cooperation with the ICC's investigation, they also pushed back hard on the home front, both politically and extra-legally. Journalists for *The Guardian* spoke with an ICC witness who admitted to receiving a US$10,000 bribe to change his story.[47] The ICC prosecutor and several human rights organizations accused the defendants of witness tampering, paying witnesses, and even having a hand in witness deaths.

Ultimately the cases against both men failed. Charges against Kenyatta were withdrawn in 2014 after the defendant traveled to The Hague for a status conference. Spinning the circumstances to his best advantage, Kenyatta stripped himself of his presidential power before leaving Kenya for The Hague, turning the presidency temporarily over to Ruto in order to travel to The Hague as a private citizen and thereby not implicate Kenya's sovereignty. Recognizing this gambit for what it was, one international law professor penned a biting blog post on "how to bet and win against the international system."[48] In 2016 the ICC dismissed its indictment against Ruto, whose trial had been suspended.[49] While the ICC's dismissal of the *Ruto* case is only valid pending further evidence, which carries the possibility of resumption should evidence be collected, this is a technicality. For practical purposes, the case against Ruto, and his co-defendant, Joshua Sang, is over, with corruption and violence having won the day over process and rule of law.

In the failed prosecutions of Kenyatta and Ruto, the ICC was summoned as a savior and transformed into a bully. Self-referral cases have provided an easy "ICC as neocolonial bully" narrative. Sometimes, ICC representatives pledge their assistance to politicians with unclean hands,[50] such as ICC prosecutor Luis Moreno-Ocampo's collaboration with Ugandan President Yoweri Museveni.[51] At other times, court representatives assert that the court will prosecute "all sides" but needs to start somewhere, and as it just so happens, it starts with the losers of a conflict. This was the case in the prosecution of Laurent Gbagbo and Charles Blé Goudé of Côte d'Ivoire. Gbagbo was president of Côte d'Ivoire from 2000 until 2010; Blé Goudé was his minister of youth.[52] In 2010 Gbagbo lost an election to Alassane Ouattara, but refused to concede power. In the resulting months of violence, more than 3,000 people were killed. Although both sides were guilty of election-related violence, ICC prosecutors charged Gbagbo with designing and executing a common plan to hold onto power through violence directed at civilians and merged his case with Blé Goudé's after the latter's arrest in 2014. Ouattara was not charged, causing frustration for many court watchers as well as victims of election violence in Côte d'Ivoire.

Adding insult to injury, after the damage meted out by the court by only investigating one side, the investigation failed: in January 2019 Gbagbo and Blé Goudé were acquitted. The acquittal did not surprise court watchers, who had followed the steadily declining case against the defendants throughout 2018. The form of the OTP's failure is still significant, however, because the court acceded to the defense's request to acquit based on a "no case to answer" motion. The prosecution has the burden of proving that the defendants, presumed innocent, are guilty. At the end of the prosecution's case, the defense can bring a "no case to answer" motion asserting that defendants *could not* be found guilty based on the evidence before the court. This is generally a hard motion to win, as the question before the court is not "will this court find the defendants not guilty?" but rather "could *no court* reasonably find the defendants guilty?" This is the motion Gbagbo's and Blé Goudé's attorneys filed when the prosecution's case ended in January 2018. Over the course of 2018, the defense and prosecution fought out the question of whether the prosecution had made a case capable of incriminating the two defendants. The January 2019 judgment answered this question in the negative. Thus, a majority of the ICC ruled not simply that Gbagbo and Blé Goudé were innocent, but rather that the prosecution had failed to make a case that would permit *any court* to convict them.

The acquittal of Gbagbo and Blé Goudé appears to indicate a more foundational collapse of international criminal law's promise to hold any and all accountable for commissions of gross violations of human rights. The central premise of international criminal law is its contestation of the absolute sovereignty of states. The post–World War II supranational system challenges sovereign states as absolute arbiters of the welfare of their citizens. The high-level cases that have collapsed at the ICC highlight the difficulties faced by institutions that rely on state cooperation to bring prosecutions; powerful figures with powerful coalitions are successfully resisting challenges to their sovereignty, even when such challenges are based on their violations of universal rights.

Conclusion

This chapter has told a story of ICC failures. Not all these problems, however, are the court's fault. The ICC is an institution guided by its member states, and some of the failures above can be attributed to lack of political, financial, and institutional rule-making support, which might have ameliorated difficulties. In some cases, there is a narrative failure that is partially attributable to the ICC's role as a court. Courts are not supposed to be political, and being political decreases their legitimacy. The ICC, like the ICTY before it, has retreated to its courtness when facing political challenge. The court's answer to critiques about its *Gbagbo-Blé Goudé* case, and wider observations that it only prosecutes rebels, is that it investigates *grave crimes*, and the question of who committed the grave crime (or what side benefited from it) is a political question outside of its purview. The ICC must necessarily lose the battle for hearts and minds that is political narrative, because to engage in this battle would threaten its legitimacy.

In 2018 I brought a group of students to The Hague to tour the ICC and other international courts. By chance, our tour overlapped with a group of young Kenyan politicians who had recently been elected and who also had come to learn about the ICC. Members of this group were surprised to learn that the *propio motu* case brought by the ICC prosecutor against Kenyan leaders was not generated by zealous prosecutorial action but rather in response to a Kenyan institutional request (the 2008 Waki Commission); they had not known this part of the story. The ICC's role in responding to a request duly made by one of its member states (Kenya) was news to them. This anecdote may go some way to explain how it is that politicians can, day to day, (i) incite genocidal-type violence,[53] (ii) share power in order to win elections, and (iii) murder and bribe individual adversaries, and pay no political price.[54] Kenyatta and Ruto controlled the narrative, and the ICC could not figure out how to compete on this level.

On the other hand, the narrative of neutrality, objectivity, and truth is a strong counternarrative, a significant advantage courts enjoy over other institutions and state actors. This is what makes the ICC's third failure, the failure of doctrine demonstrated in the *Bemba* judgment, and arguably present in *Lubanga*, so problematic. The ICC can't compete in politics, so it needs to win in legal argument, and this is an area where the ICC, and international criminal law as a field, still has much room for development.

TWO

Rejecting Liberalism in
Post-Genocide Rwanda

The small African country of Rwanda is perhaps the most concentrated modern example of the application of international criminal justice. After close to one million people were slaughtered over a few months' time in 1994, the UN Security Council created an international ad hoc tribunal, the International Criminal Tribunal for Rwanda (ICTR), to try atrocity crimes associated with the genocide. The ICTR was headquartered in neighboring Arusha, Tanzania. This tribunal, advocating liberalism in place of violent ethnonationalism, represented a multilateral effort to assist in the construction of a human rights–respecting state.

For several years, post-genocide Rwanda worked in close cooperation with the ICTR as it brought cases against mid- and high-level Hutu genocidaires. As investigations broadened to include other atrocities committed by Tutsis or against Hutus, however, the once-cooperative Rwandan government became intransigent, ceasing to permit witnesses to travel to Arusha and otherwise throwing up obstacles to the tribunal's function. Aligning itself with powerful geopolitical allies, the Rwandan government was able to remove the aggressive ICTR prosecutor, Carla Del Ponte, who had advocated, among other things, investigations of Tutsi crimes. This lack of cooperation with the tribunal on the part of Rwanda has extended to rejection of the International Criminal Court (ICC); Rwanda has not joined, and the current regime constitutes part of the East African anglophone contingent working within the African Union (AU) to encourage withdrawal from the ICC. Thus, Rwanda now categori-

cally rejects cooperation with the same forms of international criminal justice
that helped the current regime consolidate power.

Rwanda's rejection of liberal institutionalism is mostly overlooked in considering contemporary Rwanda, which is often referenced as a modern success story.[1] Paul Kagame, the leader of the Tutsi forces who ended the 1994
genocide, is an international darling, feted for overseeing an economic miracle
in Rwanda, which boasted 8 percent growth between 2001 and 2014, and has
seen impressive upsurges in primary school enrollment, life expectancy, and
gross national income.[2] The truth is darker, however; beyond the gleaming
cafes and neat sidewalks of the capital, a more insidious despotic politics is at
work.

Kagame's authoritarian state brooks no opposition. His strongest political
rival, Victoire Ingabire, was released in 2018 from a fifteen-year jail sentence,
which she was serving for the crime of "violations of genocide ideology," that
is, contesting the regime's account of the genocide.[3] Ingabire should count
herself lucky, however, as many other political actors who oppose Kagame
have been murdered.[4] Kagame won a third term as president in 2017 and is
slated to rule until 2034. While this new term violates African Union rules
on term limits, Kagame still was able to head up the organization from January 2017 to January 2018. He has received glowing reports of his "reformist"
agenda for the AU. But most relevant for our consideration are the twenty-five
years since the 1994 genocide, which have seen the Hutu-Tutsi divide remain
intact, reified by Kagame's Tutsi politics criminalizing actions such as discussion of Hutu victims, Hutu saviors, or Tutsi perpetrators. Thus, Rwanda is
challenged precisely in the normative axes that international justice is meant
to address, such as ethnic reconciliation, transparent governance, and rule of
law. Moreover, there is a disconnect between Rwandan reality and international discourse that has worked to the benefit of a character who might, if
justice were impartial, have faced trial himself.

This chapter tells a more complete story of Rwanda in order to consider
how the ICTR came to serve as a tool to consolidate Kagame's ethnicity-based
power rather than as a proponent of liberal humanism. The value of an international tribunal lies partially in its imagined immunity from local power
struggles. The story of the ICTR challenges that idea. What matters is that
beyond the frustration of investing global resources by way of a blood-thirsty
authoritarian leader, the failure to achieve transitional justice's governance
aims leaves Rwanda vulnerable to future social violence.

Rwanda's Two Genocides and Kagame's Ethnic State

There were two genocides in Rwanda. The first, the one that occupies mainstream attention, occurred in 1994, over the course of 100 days from April to June. This is the genocide of Tutsis, although it also included moderate Hutus; it is estimated that 800,000 people were murdered. This genocide was carried out by vast numbers of the population and was effectuated mostly with simple farming tools. It is the subject of Philip Gourevitch's brutally moving 1998 book, *We Wish to Inform You that Tomorrow We Will Be Killed with Our Families*, as well as popular movies like *Hotel Rwanda* (2005).

The second genocide is the genocide of Hutus in 1996–1997 (although moderate Tutsi also were targeted), perpetrated by Kagame's Rwandan Patriotic Front (RPF) and rebels from Laurent Kabila's Alliance of Democratic Forces for the Liberation of Congo-Zaire (ADFL) in the Democratic Republic of the Congo. This is sometimes called the First Congo War.[5] It is not popularly recognized as a genocide, although it was documented at the time and is a staple of area studies literature regarding Rwanda; more than 200,000 people are believed to have been killed. This second genocide has been the topic of recent literature and film, though the violence has long been recognized, documented, and discussed.[6] This second genocide is contentious, political, and often rejected as "rubbish" or "absurd," by the Rwandan political establishment, survivors of the 1994 genocide, as well as by many academics.

Genocide is both a legal and normative term. In legal parlance it means "the destruction of a group in whole or in part," and it has been recognized as a criminal act under international law since 1948.[7] The intent of group destruction is essential to the legal definition of genocide; violence must be conducted against a person based on their group identity, with the larger goal of harming the whole group. There are examples of mass violence that do not meet the definition of genocide because the group definition is not met: the class-based murder of two million Cambodians by the Khmer Rouge is one oft-cited example.[8] Thus, the UN's determination that the 200,000 Rwandans killed between 1996 and 1997 "could be characterized as crimes of genocide" should be understood to turn on legal determinations regarding the intent of the violence, as the report itself explains in paragraphs 27–33.[9]

Normatively, genocide functions as the worst and most serious violation of international humanitarian law. In the hierarchy of atrocities recognized by international criminal law, genocide is understood to be at the top.[10] It is "the crime of crimes,"[11] standing out on the hierarchy of atrocity as the most beastly form of violence that humans commit against each other. Whether this designation is warranted is outside the parameters of this chapter, though the subject forms a fascinating field of study.[12] For our purposes, it is sufficient to note that a particular element of the crime of genocide is the *group* element: atrocities committed against individuals rise to the level of genocide when those individuals are selected in order to harm the group to which they belong.

Rwanda's Cyclical Violence

The Rwandan case begins long before 1994. As Helen Epstein notes, "It is important to bear in mind that the violence was not spontaneous. It emerged from a century or more of injustice and brutality on both sides."[13] Rwanda has seen waves of ethnic-based violence and ethnic-based authoritarian governance, which helps explain both how Hutu extremists were motivated to kill Tutsis, as well as why ethnic Tutsi-based governance persists under Kagame.[14] Rwanda's international partners err when they treat the 1994 genocide as unique.

The genesis of the 1994 genocide was the downing of a French plane carrying Rwandan president Juvénal Habyarimana and Burundian president Cyprien Ntaryamira, both Hutus. The plane was shot down by two surface-to-air missiles while on approach to Kigali airport. All on board were killed, including six Rwandan and Burundian government officials and three French crew members.

Habyarimana and Ntaryamira were returning from meetings in Tanzania related to the Arusha Accords, signed in 1993 between several Hutu parties and the Tutsi RPF in order to end what had been a civil war, a conflict that had begun in 1990 when RPF forces invaded Rwanda from Uganda. Those RPF forces were comprised largely of Tutsi refugees who had been living in Uganda following the Rwandan Revolution of 1959, when Hutus had targeted ethnic Tutsi, executing them in the thousands and causing more than 300,000 to flee, most to Uganda for refuge. Paul Kagame is a product of this exodus and grew up in a refugee camp in Uganda.[15]

In the 1980s during Ugandan power contests, Kagame allied himself with Yoweri Museveni, a Ugandan military officer, and became a high-ranking military leader on the winning side when Museveni took control of the country in 1986. Kagame and fellow Rwandan Tutsis then turned their attention to Rwanda. Stationed in southern Uganda, enjoying Museveni's support, the RPF made raids into Rwanda to challenge the Hutu leadership. This became a protracted armed conflict in 1990 but ended in a stalemate until 1993 with peace accords. This was the situation in 1994, when the plane carrying the two presidents was shot down.

The question of who shot down the presidential plane remains contested. For more than a decade, the agreed line was that Hutu extremist elements were responsible. This was supported by reports concerning the original source of the missiles and evidence that extremist Hutu elements had prepared for the post-assassination response. Within a day, the moderate Hutu second in command in the Rwandan government, Agathe Uwilingiyimana, had been murdered together with ten Belgian peacekeepers assigned to protect her. The UN contingent, on site to observe processes under the peace accords, was stymied by roadblocks around Kigale, and mass killing commenced. In other words, within hours of the downing of the plane, the genocide of Tutsis by Hutu extremists was actively under way, suggesting coordination.

Many contest this interpretation, however, and lay the blame for Habyarimana's assassination on Kagame's RPF. Such a scenario can also be supported by some of the facts known. For example, the RPF itself began its advance from Uganda into Rwanda within hours of the attack, suggesting some foreknowledge. Furthermore, while violence by Hutu extremists was concentrated in the capital Kigale, the RPF avoided the city, where its intervention could have immediately saved lives, and instead focused on taking control of the country, that is, achieving its military objective. Also, with the airport under its control, the RPF refused to allow UN peacekeepers to investigate the crash site. Kagame told Romeo Dallaire, head of the UN's peacekeeping force in the country, "The international community is looking at sending an intervention force on humanitarian grounds. But for what reason? If an intervention force is sent to Rwanda, we will fight it."[16] This fuels suspicion that the RPF had something to hide.

While she wryly notes that this question of which side shot down the plane can lead to riots at academic conferences, scholar Helen Epstein cites several reasons why she is more convinced that the attack was made by Kagame's RPF, including the source of weapons used (Soviet-made weapons sold to Uganda in the 1980s) and control of the area where the attack originated. Epstein also cites five investigations, where only two absolve Kagame's regime of responsibility, both of which were made by Kagame's regime.[17] Regardless, for our purposes, it is less important to determine responsibility for the attack than to observe the structures of obfuscation and nationalism that have surrounded the question of responsibility. The factual question regarding the downing of the plane has now become so partisan that to raise the question is already to indicate which side of the fight one falls on.

From Genocide to Kagame's Presidency: Taking Sides

From April through July 1994, mass slaughter was effectuated through organized killing groups called Interahamwe, made up of extremist Hutus and their supporters. In Kigale as well as around the country, in towns, villages, and churches, groups of Hutu exterminators rounded up Tutsi and moderate Hutu for execution. People were gathered at roadblocks, in town squares, and in their homes. In some areas, locals were told to either join in the killing or be killed themselves. The killing was treated as "work" and often performed during daylight hours, between 8 a.m. and 4 p.m.[18]

It took three months for Kagame's forces to bring the Hutu genocide to a halt and seize control of the country. The UN, present in small numbers in the country in relation to the 1993 peace accords, was prohibited from intervening and thus largely unable to mitigate the violence.[19] The RPF's takeover of Kigale in July 1994 resulted in a mass flight of Hutus, those who had participated in the genocide as well as others who feared reprisals, into neighboring Zaire (now Democratic Republic of the Congo), where hundreds of thousands set up refugee camps. Those camps housed civilians, but also hosted militia members, who took over control of the camps and used them as bases to make forays into Rwanda and perpetrate violence against Tutsis and the Kagame-led government.[20] During these events, it is estimated that the RPF itself killed between 25,000 and 45,000 people.[21] These numbers are contested by the RPF, which restricted access to the territory it held, making facts hard to establish.

The RPF-dominated government brought Paul Kagame to the presidency in 2000, where he has remained ever since, having been recently reelected in 2017 with 99 percent of the vote in an election plagued by irregularities. He now ranks among the top ten richest presidents in Africa, with an estimated net worth of half a billion dollars.[22]

Numbers relating to the loss and violence in Rwanda are generally uncontested, however:

- between 800,000 to 1,000,000 perished during the 100-day genocide in April–July 1994, and

- between 200,000 and 500,000 civilians were killed in the ensuing years as the RPF and RPF-backed militias chased down and exterminated Hutus who had fled Rwanda.[23]

While those are the facts in this case, the genocide still generates significantly distinctive perspectives on the violence and its perpetrators. Battle lines in the discussion have been drawn and are vigorously defended, often quite staunchly by individuals with no personal stake in the game. Two recent showdowns are illustrative: the first was fought out in the open in the mainstream press and concerns a BBC documentary, and the second was fought in more specialized literature and reveals deep divides in academia.

In 2014 the BBC released a one-hour documentary, *Rwanda's Untold Story*, which set off an avalanche of protest in the media and in Rwanda. As its name suggests, the documentary sought to challenge some elements of the mainstream narrative regarding the Rwanda genocide, specifically the nature of the Interahamwe and Hutu power movements, particularly what percentage were trained killers; the number of Tutsi killed (they claimed the film misrepresented and "minimized" this number); and who bore responsibility for the downing of President Habyarimana's plane, which initiated the genocide (as noted, a contentious topic). Responding to the documentary, thirty-eight area scholars and activists, led by Linda Melvern, published a letter in protest.[24] They argued the BBC had been "recklessly irresponsible" to air the program, because it "fueled genocide denial" and "emboldened the genocidaires, all their supporters and those who collaborate with them."[25] In particular, they took issue with the three claims the program explored, which they categorized as not "untold" but rather old and jaded news. In Rwanda, Kagame's regime took a strong position against the documentary, suspending the BBC's broadcast license in the country in October 2014 and opening a judicial inquiry into criminal liability in relation to the broadcast. This resolute stance, using all the powers of government at its disposal to silence dissent, is a common theme in Rwanda under Kagame.

Immediately following the October 2014 protest letter, University of Antwerp professor Filip Reyntjens published a blunt response challenging the protesters' claims that the BBC made "untenable" arguments and generally defending the BBC's right to air the program. He began with an ad hominem critique of the thirty-eight signatories, only three of whom were academics. Of Melvern, he said she "calls herself 'Professor,' but she is not; she has merely been an honorary professor at the University of Wales Aberystwyth." Reyntjens dismissed the other non-academic signatories as people who "have either shown interest in Rwanda in the past or played a role there, or have a sectoral expertise, e.g. in genocide studies or international criminal law. Some are activists with a record of support for the Rwandan government."[26] These fighting words achieved their desired effect, and as of this writing, the controversy continues. Melvern's latest contribution to this volley is her 2020 book, *Intent to Deceive: Denying the Rwandan Genocide* (Verso).

Melvern has been a protagonist in a less public but no less vituperative debate about facts and narratives in Rwanda, where skirmishes have taken place in the pages of *Human Rights Quarterly*, a leading academic journal. In 2016 Notre Dame professor Luc Reydams wrote an article arguing that the narrative of violence in Rwanda should be traced back to a single 1994 report produced a few months after the genocide by a nongovernmental organization based in London with two staff members, Africa Rights.[27] He argues that Africa Rights was co-opted by the RPF, acting essentially as its mouthpiece, as a means of winning the peace. This is significant because the narrative, incidents, and individuals named in the Africa Rights report went on to form the backbone of the ICTR prosecution of the genocide. These allegations provoked outrage among some area scholars and regime proponents.[28] In 2018 Melvern was among a group who wrote a rebuttal in the *Human Rights Quarterly*, where they argued that Reydams's critique was erroneous and unprofessional.[29]

Alex de Waal, one of the two Africa Rights team members behind the 1994 report who now teaches at Tufts University, has himself weighed in on the process of collecting and producing information dispassionately and objectively. In a 2016 article de Waal appears to admit to some of the observations of structural bias Reydams identifies, such as the pressure on NGO organizations to demonstrate competence via access to locals and information in the competitive pursuit of funding for human rights activities.[30]

For those of us without a dog in this fight, these skirmishes are nonetheless significant, because they demonstrate not only how complex and contested the facts are, but also the ways this messiness is operationalized in service to particular interests and perspectives. The two contests about accuracy and the Rwanda genocide referenced above showcase extreme partisanship, where to ask a question or recognize a perspective is already to align oneself with those deemed heroes or villains. This is an extreme example of the kind of siloed thinking the sociologist Joachim Savelsberg identifies as "competing representations" of human rights violations between different actors.[31] Even when groups share the same norms and the same general goals, their particular resources, interests, and strengths may encourage very disparate assessments of how to understand, or when to contest, a set of facts.

ICL and Reconciliation

As discussed in the book's introduction, international criminal law is applied as a transitional justice mechanism on the theory that constructing certain kinds of violence as illegal and illegitimate can be an effective method to combat ethnic, racist, discriminatory, and otherwise non-rights-respecting governance. Genocide, war crimes, and crimes against humanity are, in this construction, illegitimate forms of exercising government control, no matter how useful they might be for one side. International humanitarian law (the law of war, which regulates what kinds of conduct in war constitute war crimes) rejects Clausewitz's (1989) total war formulation—that in pursuit of victory, all is permitted. International criminal law makes prosecutions of violations of humanitarian law, as well as other, similarly impermissible collective government action (crimes against humanity, mass violence punishable even outside of war, and genocide) punishable against individuals involved in those illegal acts. It is built on a humanist platform, where the central question is what act, with what purpose, was committed by representatives of the state or other collective power. In this way, international criminal law supports progressive ideals of rights-based liberal governance by rejecting ethnic or other group characteristics as rationales for state violence. In other words, international criminal law is in principle not concerned with who is killed but rather with the impermissible forms of violence themselves. This is understood to be a means of promoting social reconciliation because it places a humanist conception of people in place of an ethnic or nationalist conception. The ideal is that we can all agree on certain forms of violence that are impermissible regardless of who is victimized by them, and that this shared understanding can build our community.

In the aftermath of the wars of dissolution in the former Yugoslavia, a Serb and Bosnian Muslim film-making team produced a documentary that perfectly encapsulates this sought-after spirit of international criminal law and the tribunals practicing it. The documentary featured interviews with people in the two areas that had been the subject of ICTY prosecution at the time of filming: one a town in central Bosnia, where Bosnian Muslims had run a small camp beating and torturing tens of Bosnian Serbs, and one a town in northeastern Bosnia, where Bosnian Serbs ran a successful ethnic cleansing and genocide campaign that killed or otherwise removed tens of thousands of Bosnian Muslims. The documentary featured interviews with people who had been subjected to state-sponsored violence and deliberately removed signs and information that would allow the viewer to categorize the ethnicity of the victims. Demographically, the violence in Bosnia should be understood as violence against Bosnian Muslims, who were disproportionately represented in victim numbers from the war, targeted by both Serbs and Croats. Likewise, Croat-sponsored violence did not reach the same genocidal proportions as Serb-sponsored violence. Yet the purpose of the film was to ignore the demographic reality of who the victims were by the numbers and instead focus on individual victimization.[32]

A similar focus on individuality and rights is at work in a documentary, *The Uncondemned*, made about the Akeyesu case, discussed further below. There, rape survivors testified before the ICTR. Their identities were not divulged to the court to protect them from retaliatory harm, ranging from social stigma to violence. The documentary follows the work of young American and European lawyers and investigators as they decided to include rape as part of genocide charges against a perpetrator, and the story is in many ways about these young lawyers constructing a new institution, the ICTR. At the end of the film, however, several of the rape survivors, discussing the testimony they gave before the ICTR, announce their names. The point the documentary is making is that these individuals do not need to hide in anonymity; we can all, beginning with the women announcing their identities, recognize that the violence committed against them was criminal.

The above recounts the normative understanding regarding what trials, built on objective criminal definitions, are designed and argued to achieve. The reality is, of course, more complex, and many elements of it—particularly the instrumentalization of Rwandan rape victims to build international criminal law doctrine—are quite problematic. The point is that the empowerment of the individual as a rights-possessing being regardless of ethnicity, sex, religious belief, and so on, is fundamental to the reconciliatory work imagined for international criminal law. This normative understanding imagines that this exists both at the level of the individuals impacted, who are seeking justice, as well as for those observing the process, who recognize justice served. Under this theory, trials represent a shared understanding of justice (or, alternately, criminality) that is designed to create community.

The ICTR

Rwanda represents a significant investment and experiment in modern transitional justice. Following the 1994 genocide, the UN Security Council established an ad hoc tribunal in Arusha, Tanzania—with Appellate Chambers in The Hague—to hear crimes associated with the genocide.[33] (The Security

Council, at the same time, was involved in setting up an ad hoc tribunal to address violence in the former Yugoslavia.) The ICTR functioned from 1995 through 2015 and heard fifty-five cases. In all, ninety-three individuals were indicted in connection with the genocide. More than its sister institution for the former Yugoslavia, the ICTR received a mixed review from proponents of international criminal law, its practice marred by inefficiency, corruption, nepotism, and overt politicization.[34]

The ICTR was established with a recognizable reconciliation and transitional justice mandate. The statute specifically articulates that the UN Security Council was:

> *convinced* that in the particular circumstances of Rwanda, the prosecution of persons responsible for serious violations of international humanitarian law would enable this aim to be achieved and would contribute to the process of national reconciliation and to the restoration and maintenance of peace.[35]

This language is exemplary of transitional justice ideology. Unlike the statute governing the ICTR's sister tribunal, the ICTY, the ICTR statute explicitly considers the goal of reconciliation within the work of the institution. The ICTR statute makes explicit the transitional justice goals underwriting the institution.

In 1995 the seat of the tribunal in Arusha was formally established by UN resolution. This brief, five-line resolution specifically made note of "the willingness of the Government of Rwanda to cooperate with the Tribunal."[36] In 1998 the ICTR was expanded with a third trial chamber,[37] signaling full-steam ahead for the use of the tribunal, and UN resources, to prosecute perpetrators of violations of international humanitarian law in Rwanda.

The first judgment rendered by the ICTR was the momentous and celebrated *Prosecutor v. Akayesu* (1998) case.[38] Akayesu was the mayor of a medium-sized town who came to the ICTR's attention because his name was on a list produced by the RPF government following the war.[39] Although Akeyesu originally resisted calls to participate in the genocide,[40] under pressure from the ruling Hutus, he eventually changed course and ordered the police to capture RPF sympathizers, that is, Tutsi: the ICTR prosecutor alleged that over 2,000 people were murdered in the commune over which Akeyesu presided.[41]

At trial, it was additionally revealed that over a period of many weeks during the genocide, women were held in the town hall compound and repeatedly raped. Based on this information, and armed with legal memoranda regarding the possible legal characterization of sexual violence during war, the prosecution team eventually charged Akeyesu with using rape as a form of genocide, as it was perpetrated with the aim of destroying the life of the victim.

The judges agreed, and in 1998, in the first case produced by the ICTR, the judges found Akeyesu guilty of rape that constituted genocide. The *Akayesu* case found that rape constituted genocide, based on rape's potential to destroy those against whom it is perpetrated, even when they are not killed. This was also in addition to other more traditional understandings of rape as it related to genocide, such as children born of rape belonging to a different ethnic group and the group's destruction in this way.[42] This creative and progressive application of legal principles, much celebrated by proponents of international criminal law at the time and since, has never been repeated.

Other significant decisions by the ICTR include the 1998 guilty plea regarding the genocide of Jean Kambanda,[43] the 2003 judgments against the founders of Radio Mille Collines and several newspapers, all of whom helped incite the genocide,[44] and the 2008 conviction of Colonel Theoneste Bagosora, identified as the "kingpin"[45] or central organizer of the genocide.[46]

The 2011 appellate opinion regarding Bagosora's case is a good example of the strife and conflict that characterized ICTR practice and helps explain the critical or otherwise muted reception to the tribunal's work among some legal scholars and academics. The appeal was heard by five judges who issued five separate opinions. The appeals judgment affirmed and dismissed counts against the two appellants, reducing Bagosora's sentence from life imprisonment to thirty-five years, and Vincent Nsengiyumva's life sentence to fifteen years, which meant he was released immediately. Additionally, Judges Meron and Robinson appended a joint dissenting opinion, Judge Güney appended a partially dissenting opinion, Judge Pocar appended a dissenting opinion, and Judges Pocar and Liu appended a joint dissenting opinion. Since unanimity among judicial voices helps build institutional legitimacy, five opinions from five judges presented uncertainty and impacts rule-of-law acceptance.

The ICTR and Reconciliation

Throughout its practice, the ICTR declined to indict and prosecute Tutsis but not for lack of evidence of Tutsi crimes. The 1994 UN Commission report on the genocide found "extensive evidence of systematic killings and persecution" committed by Kagame's Rwandan Patriotic Front.[47] Richard Goldstone, the first prosecutor for the ICTR, maintained that his office did not investigate RPF crime because the "magnitude" of such crimes was not at the same level as Hutu genocide.[48] Subsequent prosecutors, Louise Arbour and

Carla Del Ponte, began investigating Tutsi crime, but with great care because such investigations brought considerable risk of reprisal from the Kagame government.[49] Relatively early in her tenure, Del Ponte, known for her tenacious approach, worked from investigations secretly begun by Arbour before her, to begin compiling reports of Tutsi-committed atrocities in preparation for bringing an indictment.[50] Such atrocities muddled the narrative of Hutu monstrosity and Tutsi victimhood and could, potentially, lead to Kagame himself. For her efforts, Del Ponte was eventually removed from office in 2003. Done under cover, the official story for the departure cited an excess of work that led to the severing of the joint prosecutorial capacity between the two ad hoc tribunals (ICTR and ICTY), relegating Del Ponte to the ICTY alone.[51] Del Ponte was replaced by Hassan Bubacar Jallow, a Ghanian who was content not to pressure the ruling regime.

The ICTR ceased indictments in 2004 and closed its doors in 2015. This followed a similar pattern for the ICTY, and the cessation of indictments is largely attributable to weariness with the cost and disappointing returns associated with ICTs. During this period no Tutsis were tried, and the investigations made into atrocities committed by the RPF bore no fruit. In his 2008 book, Victor Peskin considered the problems of prosecuting a conflict's victors as a new form of the old "victor's justice" adage.[52] Prosecuting the winners of international conflict comes with particular difficulties, chiefly that such victors control access to necessary information and are often ill-disposed to make that information available.

The Kagame regime also exerted pressure in what might be considered more subtle ways. Rwanda effectively used cooperation with the tribunal as a bargaining chip in pressing an agenda that would keep considerations of violence in Rwanda one-sided.[53] This pressure was institutionally effective, due to the particular existential challenges that face international tribunals; without defendants in the dock, international criminal tribunals lose their raison d'être. A non-cooperative Kagame not providing necessary resources (even with regard to Hutu genocidaires) could help shut the ICTR down. In this regard, international organizations are as hampered as domestic institutions might be in attempting to prosecute state-sponsored atrocity.

Gacaca and State Capture

International justice was necessarily quite limited. Although a few cases were referred to the Rwanda judicial system from the ICTR, the domestic system was also inadequate to meet the demand, as it is estimated that at least

100,000 people actively took part in the genocide. Thus, the government set up a system of local tribunals, the "gacaca" courts. These courts were based on traditional dispute resolution practices, although in their government form, they could hear cases of genocide and mete out punishment. The approximately 12,000 gacaca courts ran from 2005 to 2012 and heard 1.2 million cases.[54]

There is a great deal of literature addressing this novel, creative reimagining of local justice.[55] The gacaca system was a traditional form of community management (the word translates to something like "on the grass") that was repurposed to hear cases from the genocide. The gacaca process is generally received as "mixed."[56] On the one hand, there is much to celebrate in the creation of locally organized and understood processes, particularly in colonial contexts where law, power, and development have traditionally been imposed from the top. On the other hand, the processes themselves often failed rule-of-law fairness criteria. The gacaca dispute system as traditionally employed was for the resolution of local property or contract disputes, and not, as it was engaged by the Kagame government, for the resolution of genocide-related crimes. Judges were not trained in fair trial procedures, and defendants also suffered from a lack of procedural protection. Furthermore, no allegations of RPF-related crime were permitted before gacaca courts, which were constructed specifically to hear cases involving the Hutu-generated genocide.

Nicola Palmer argues that the gacaca system served a different purpose than the ICTR and local criminal courts and should be examined as part of a tripartite transitional justice story that includes the ICTR, Rwandan criminal courts, and gacaca processes.[57] For example, she argues that gacaca courts should be seen as a response to international condemnation of Rwanda criminal justice, which sentenced several defendants to death in 1998.[58] These sentences, which were carried out, came months before the first ICTR decision and brought swift, negative reactions from international observers.

For our purposes, it is sufficient to note that local responses to genocide did not diverge from the local political capture of the ICTR. Area scholars add nuance to the charge of authoritarianism in contemporary Rwandan politics, considering the role that ethnicity has traditionally played in centralizing power.[59] These interesting points do not take away from the overall message, however, that investment in political liberalism in the form of rule-of-law institutions had been captured, and in turn rejected, in Kagame's Rwanda.

Rejecting Liberalism in Kagame's Rwanda

In an article published in 2008, Helen Hintjens described a post-genocide Rwanda where:

> political identities have been reconstructed since the genocide, especially from above. History, law and politics are examined, as central instruments in government efforts to construct a new Rwandan society and ensure that genocide will "never again" be possible. Evidence suggests that inequalities in income and land distribution have grown rapidly since 1994. At the same time, the poor and marginalized often find it difficult to openly express their views, including their political identities outside of officially circumscribed spaces and categories. Debates continue around numbers of victims and perpetrators, and new inter-elite conflicts have emerged along language lines.[60]

Today, the situation described by Hintjens has grown, if anything, worse. Susan Thomson provides the latest, very thorough challenge to the popular wisdom of Rwanda's recovery. Thomson tells the story of how "the PRF has created a precarious peace, one that has consolidated its power and authority at the expense of other ways of imagining Rwanda's shared future and developing its people."[61]

The current wave of Kagame critique has gained significant attention in popular press circles, particularly in Judi Rever's 2018 book.[62] Rever, a journalist who traveled through Rwanda following the genocide, is a proponent of the two genocides theory, where the first was perpetrated by the Hutus against Tutsis (as well as moderate Hutus, although this element is not permissible under the RPF narrative) and the second was perpetrated by the RPF against Hutus and others, with many of the killings occurring outside Rwanda, in the lawless and unsupervised hinterlands of Kabila's Congo. Skipping the well-known story of western intransigence regarding the first genocide, Rever traces western support for Kagame's genocide. Written decades after some of the violence she witnessed firsthand, Rever does not reveal unknown facts.[63] Rather, she offers further support, and chilling details, to an already known story. The pressing question that arises is: why don't these known facts impact the accepted narrative of Rwandan violence? Why does Kagame continue to enjoy the support of western states, which have sanctioned him in even his most anti-democratic measures (his third-term appointment, putting him in power through 2034; his jailing of opposition political leaders)?

The short answer would appear to be that Kagame is supported because Kigali is clean and modern.[64] Visitors to Rwanda, most of whom never leave the capital city, enjoy the smooth roads, the tidy city center, and the prevalence of wifi. Corporations seeking to invest enjoy modern legal forms. Modern Kigali obscures the reality of Rwanda outside of Kigali.

A more theoretically complex answer is offered by development scholars like Tim Kelsall, who argue that imperfect democracy may be a necessary element of economic development. In his book Kelsall argues in favor of what he identifies as "neo-patrimonial" governance as beneficial to the state.[65] This governance comprises favoritism, in families, friends, ethnic groups, and so on, and permits personal enrichment, that is, what liberal governance labels fraud and corruption. Kelsall, however, shows how these methods can result in state growth even while individuals are enriched, and he argues for expanding the categories in which we adjudicate what constitutes the public interest.

Courts Pushing Back, with Mixed Results

This chapter has considered the disappointing track record of the ICTR in relation to a more complete accounting of atrocities in Rwanda and a more vigorous foundation for liberal democracy in the country. There are, regardless, other courts pushing back against Kagame's narrative, with greater and lesser success.

In 2006 French investigating magistrate Jean-Louis Bruguière completed a several-year investigation of the downing of President Habyarimana's plane and concluded that Kagame's RPF was responsible.[66] Judge Bruguière issued nine international arrest warrants for people in Kagame's inner circle.[67] Immunity guarantees for leaders prevented an arrest warrant against Kagame; Bruguière urged the ICTR to indict Kagame, since the ICTR was not bound by immunity provisions.[68] This did not happen.

The Bruguière indictments dramatically soured relations between Rwanda and France; Kagame announced that France itself had participated in the genocide and opened his own inquiry, which unsurprisingly cleared the RPF of all wrongdoing in 2009.[69] And while the case moved ahead slowly and contentiously in France, it ultimately was not able to challenge the dominant narrative of the Kagame regime; on December 21, 2018, an investigative judge determined that there was insufficient evidence to support Kagame's involvement with the downed plane. Civil parties appealed, but on July 3, 2020, the appeals court dismissed the case. While the families have promised to further appeal this decision, it seems likely that the investigation is finished in France.

South African courts have investigated political violence aimed at former Kagame associates, and here the successes are greater, though less publicized, than those of the Bruguière investigation in France. In 2014 four individuals (a Rwandan national and three Tanzanians) were found guilty of the 2010 attempted murder of Kagame's former aid, General Faustin Kayumba Nyamwasa.[70] While the individuals were found guilty of the attempted murder, the violence was not attributed to Kagame's regime. Meanwhile, the 2013 strangulation murder of Kagame's former intelligence chief, Patrick Karegeya, in an upscale Johannesburg hotel on New Year's Eve, remains unresolved; a prominent South African prosecutor has recently resumed calls for resolution of the crime.[71]

In 2017 the African Union's regional human rights court, the African Court on Human and Peoples' Rights (ACtHPR), ruled in favor of Victoire Ingabire, jailed in 2010 for the crime of genocide denial and sentenced to fifteen years of prison. Ingabire, an opposition politician, had returned to Rwanda in 2010 to register her party and run against Kagame. She was prosecuted for campaign speeches she gave that were critical of the regime's reconciliation policies. The ACtHPR found that this prosecution violated Ingabire's freedom of expression and that Rwanda had acted impermissibly against her, later assessing reparations against Rwanda in her favor. In 2018 Ingabire was released from prison although threats of violence against her and her aides and supporters, as discussed above, continue.

While Ingabire triumphed in her case against Rwanda, the fallout was damaging: Rwanda withdrew from the treaty that allows individuals to bring cases to the ACtHPR. Although the ACtHPR was able to hear Ingabire's case because her complaint was filed before the withdrawal, future complaints will not, as things stand, be possible.

Conclusion

Post-genocide Rwanda has been hailed as a miracle of modernization. It is true that under Paul Kagame, whose armies swept in from Uganda to stop the 1994 genocide, war has not returned. This seems, to some, ample evidence that the horrors of the 1994 genocide are truly past and represent no present threat. These statistics are often marshaled in support of the argument that Rwanda is successfully transitioning from a backward, corrupt, undeveloped state to a modern, democratic, rights-respecting state. By these statistics, and set against the backdrop of the horror of the 1994 genocide, contemporary Rwanda is transitioning from poverty, lawlessness, and violence to representative government, peace, and prosperity. Such transitional turning points are the aims and rationale behind the implementation of transitional justice initiatives, including criminal prosecutions under international criminal law.

Yet, as this chapter has demonstrated, western intervention in Rwanda and support for Kagame's regime have worked against the professed goals of transitional justice, as evidenced by the political situation in Rwanda following the genocide and through to today. After the Rwandan genocide, credible challenges have been mounted to counter the official version of the genocide that Hutu, and only Hutu, perpetrators committed the crime, the Tutsi were victims, and the RPF saviors. As noted above, the UN Expert Report prepared for the Security Council, even in 1994, noted systemic, RPF-organized violence. Waves of assessments critical of Kagame and his forces have followed that report, including a series of critiques ten years after the genocide,[72] and yet another wave in the past few years.[73] Studies of refugee populations outside of Rwanda challenge simplistic perpetrator-victim binaries.[74] This critical literature often references violence in pre-genocide Rwanda and the role played in Rwandan politics by neighboring countries. In other words, the Rwanda genocide did not occur in a vacuum, and it was not as binary as represented by Kagame and the RPF.

I have reviewed the problematic realities of celebrated authoritarian rule in Rwandan in light of the transitional justice ideology that involved western post-genocidal engagement and aid efforts. External intervention, chiefly in the form of the creation of the ICTR, did not present the imagined counterweight to authoritarian governance and anti-democratic rulership.

We are left with a series of puzzling questions regarding how to understand this failure. The officially professed narrative regarding Rwanda is wrong; all parties involved, from the beginning, know it is erroneous: why then such silence? The officially professed narrative of Rwanda is enforced through authoritarian measures, and thus the official narrative of Rwanda is a story of further human rights abuses and bad governance. Judicial institutions are understood to help bring clarity regarding crimes and their perpetrators, yet in the case of Rwanda, neither state nor international procedures have made much headway: what does this signify? Chapters following will consider some of these questions in relation to other institutions.

THREE

"Hybrid Justice" and
the Trial of a Chadian Dictator

The group gathered in Dakar's courthouse on April 2017 to hear the appeals judgment in the case against Hissène Habré was a who's-who of international criminal justice: Reed Brody of Human Rights Watch, who spearheaded the international campaign to bring Habré to justice, working relentlessly over twenty years; Stephen Rapp, U.S. ambassador at large for war crimes; Jaqueline Moudeïna, counsel to one of the victims' groups and a storied figure, the first female lawyer in Chad, and a longtime advocate for the powerless; as well as local and international human rights NGO officials and government representatives. All milled about in the aisles on the right side of the impressive court chamber of the Palais de Justice de Dakar, Dakar's district court, which could easily accommodate 500 people seated. I and my two co-researchers were there to follow the trial for a book we were writing.[1] After saying our hellos, we chose to sit on the left side of the room since it was far less crowded. This was the "defense" side and we had a clear view of the raised dais, where members of the prosecution team, the three presiding appeals judges, and administrative clerks of the court were to sit. Habré's *commis d'office*, who the defense lawyers appointed when his selected lawyers opted not to participate in what they called an illegitimate trial, sat in front of us. Habré's French attorney, François Serres, part of his selected team who had refused to participate in any element of the investigation or trial, paced on the sidelines by the entryway; after the appeals decision was read, he would spring into action granting interviews to assembled press. In the busy melee, where pickpockets successfully worked the crowd, the defendant, Hissène Habré, was noticeably absent.

The written judgment wasn't available that day: the Chambres Africaines Extraordinaires (CAE), an ad hoc, hybrid tribunal set up to try atrocities committed under Habré's 1982–1990 rule in Chad, was working toward a set of predetermined deadlines, and today was the due date of the appeal. The judges' contracts were to end, and the tribunal architecture itself was set to dissolve. The 300-page written judgment, produced by judges and their clerks, came only several weeks later. Instead, the chief judge read a summary of the appeals chamber's findings, which upheld the trial chamber's ruling on all but one ground, and left the trial court's sentence—life in prison—untouched.

Habré's conviction was generally received as a triumph for victims, Senegal's judicial institutions, and international criminal justice. This chapter examines these conclusions with a critical eye. Earlier chapters have discussed how particular interests shape justice mechanisms and how those interests are reflected in the workings of the institutions studied. The Hissène Habré affair complicates interest analysis as it demonstrates how "interest" is differently defined for local and international actors. Here, "interest" finds a key middle ground between the local (complex, lived, often inscrutable to outsiders) and the international (general, bird's-eye view).[2] This chapter considers the production of "professionalized" interest in the Habré procedure and considers what it may mean in the pantheon of international criminal justice institutions across Africa.

The following will set the scene beginning with Habré's authoritarian regime, its fall, and how the violence on citizens came to be heard by a specially designed hybrid court. Then I explore three central ideas that trace confluent axes in this discussion of what to do with Habré regarding his crimes:

- universal jurisdiction—the argument that crimes universally recognized as criminal, that is, atrocity crimes, may be prosecuted by any court, not only courts with specialized, clearly articulated jurisdiction over them, such as the International Criminal Court (ICC), ad hoc tribunals, and so forth;

- the rise in popularity of hybrid courts—courts that blend, both procedurally and doctrinally, international and local practice; and

- sovereign immunity—the protection against prosecution afforded to those individuals who represent a state that makes international statecraft possible, discussed at length in the first chapter.

I then examine the work of the hybrid court at issue. While the CAE was established to try atrocities committed under Habré's regime, in the end it focused on the Chadian president himself. The reader will recall previous discussions regarding the indefensibility, from a rule-of-law perspective, of constructing an institution to try a particular individual rather than a particular crime. The conclusion considers how interest is complicated in the Habré affair, where both a well-running court and a clear political reality (those out of power are legally vulnerable) vie for pride of place as reflected in the CAE experience.

Habré's Crimes and Eventual Prosecution

Chad, a former French colony liberated in 1958, is a huge, sparsely populated and desperately poor African country with a diverse population. Hissène Habré ruled Chad from 1982 to 1990. Originally from a poor northern region, Habré was spotted by a French commander and given a scholarship to study in Paris at Sciences Po, a prestigious academy for political science. On returning to Chad, Habré led a rebellion against the government, part of the fractious post-independence scramble for power in the 1970s. Habré's rebels famously kidnapped three European scientists in 1975 and held them for ransom; the hostages were eventually freed through intervention by Muammar Gaddafi in Libya, Habré's longtime enemy.[3]

Habré maintained his hold on power through support from the United States and France, which backed him in the fight against Gaddafi, sending money, troops, and training so that Habré's forces could contain Gaddafi in the north. Always on the lookout for spies and plots, Habré ran an authoritarian police state and deputized an institution of special police, the Documentation and Security Directorate (DDS), which reported directly to him. The DDS picked up whomever they pleased for interrogation and detained prisoners indefinitely. Many prisoners were tortured, using techniques perfected by the DDS, and many died. The regime's most infamous prison was *la piscine* (the pool). This former swimming pool that had once entertained French military officers and their families was covered with a cement roof, after which prisoners were stuffed into cells so crowded that it was impossible to sit or lie down. Under the desert sun, the heat inside was intense, and conditions led to loss of life. Prisoners reported that the dead were left in cells for days.[4]

The purpose of Habré's police state was to maintain his hold on power domestically and to stymie expansion attempts by Libya, the aggressor to the north. Over the course of Habré's rule, the DDS targeted ethnic groups in

Chad as they became associated with potential violence against the regime. Habré also conducted military operations to maintain power, the most infamous of which is known as Black September, in 1984, where villages were attacked and civilians massacred. The commander in charge of this campaign was Idriss Déby, at the time Habré's right-hand man.

In the late 1980s, Déby fell out with Habré and retreated to Sudan where he raised an army. He then deposed Habré in 1990 and ruled Chad until his unexpected death in a rebel skirmish in northeastern Chad in April 2021. Déby had been a significant force in the campaign to try Habré for his crimes, and there is a particular irony in that it was Déby who oversaw Black September, one of the central war crimes for which Habré is known.[5] Déby also profited handsomely from his time in government and consistently ranked in the top ten of Africa's richest leaders. He has been succeeded by his son.

When Déby ousted Habré in 1990, the deposed leader fled to Senegal on a government plane with a sizeable portion of the Chadian treasury. Senegal granted him asylum, and he set up house in Dakar's posh Ouakam neighborhood.

Back in Chad, Déby took up power under a justice and rule-of-law platform. One of Déby's first acts of office was to appoint a "truth commission" to investigate Habré's misdeeds.[6] But this commission was under-equipped in manpower and materials; its two allocated vehicles, for example, could not drive on country roads and were promptly stolen and recovered only months later, making it essentially impossible for the commissioners to investigate outside the capital, N'Djaména. The commission conducted interviews with victims in the only premises it could find, which unfortunately were Habré's DDS offices, a fact that undoubtedly contributed to victims' initial unwillingness to come forward. It was also, of course, precariously situated politically, charged with investigating violations of human rights in a state that continued to violate those rights. For example, lead commissioner Judge Mahamat Hassan Abakar reports that in 1991 Déby began using *la piscine*, the horrific symbol of Habré's worst prisoner abuses, as a prison again. Abakar reports that he wrote to Déby, demanding that the prison be retired and that Déby agreed.[7]

For all these reasons it is particularly remarkable that the commission produced and published a report that we can read today. The commission acquired access to victims and abusers in the Habré regime: ultimately, it interviewed hundreds of victims and more than forty Habré-era abusers still serving in government, a direct challenge to Déby's rule-of-law platform. It also listed "the most feared torturers" by name. For these reasons, Abakar reports that Déby did not favor publishing the commission's report. Fearing the commission's work would be in vain if the report was not published, Abakar privately released the report into the public realm.

The report found Habré guilty of several violations of international humanitarian law, including genocide.[8] The materials gathered by the truth commission continue in large part to constitute the evidence against Habré. For example, the commission found that Habré's regime had killed 40,000 people. It made this determination based on 3,700 verified deaths, which the commission, without giving a basis, determined represented "about 10 percent of Habré's actual damage" and then rounded up.[9] This estimate of the damage of Habré's regime has never been challenged or verified, served as an estimate during Habré's trial before the CAE,[10] and has now claimed an unchallenged position in the cannon. This number, however, is simply an estimate based on what Akabar himself acknowledges were arbitrary determinations of reasonableness.[11] In truth, we will never likely know how many people Habré's regime killed, either as prisoners or as soldiers or civilians on battlefields. Déby's appointed truth commission likewise determined that 200,000 people had been tortured by Habré's regime. But like the number of fatalities, this number is based on very imprecise estimates. Like the number of fatalities, the actual number may be higher or lower than that reported; we do not know.

When Déby took over Chad, he promised a more respectful state than his predecessor's, with rule of law at the center of statecraft. But little suggests this has happened.[12] Until the CAE put Habré on trial and Déby risked having his own practices revealed, Déby appeared to engage in many of the same practices, run by the same people, as Habré had. In late 2014, as Habré's trial was to begin in Dakar, Déby's regime put twenty-one defendants from the Habré-DDS era on trial in Chad. These were the first prosecutions of DDS actors under the Déby regime, and the timing was not accidental: under Chadian law, convicted persons cannot testify before a court, which suggests that the timing of these trials was related to obstructing the defendants from testifying before the CAE.[13] Following the CAE's successful conviction of Habré, reports have emerged that some of the Habré-era collaborators jailed in Chad in 2015 have been released, although Chad denies these allegations.[14]

Last, while Déby waited to try Habré's associates until the eleventh hour, he was a bit more aggressive with Habré himself. Recall that Déby's first act in office was to create a truth commission to adjudicate Habré and his regime.

Déby continuously pursued extradition of Habré from Senegal to Chad. In 2008 the criminal court in N'Djaména tried Habré *in absentia* and sentenced him to death for crimes against humanity.

Utopian Dreaming: Bringing Universal Jurisdiction to Africa

After fleeing to Dakar in 1990, Hissène Habré kept a low profile as a private citizen. Ensconced in his green, leafy neighborhood in the center of the city, he took a second wife, had children, and was active in his local mosque. He took up living a life that many post-power ex-dictators enjoy, at least those who escape death or imprisonment by the incoming regime

All the while, his victims kept pushing for his regime's crimes to be recognized and for his trial. This was not without risk at home in Chad, where Déby might talk the talk of democratic leadership, but where his walk was to continue the repressive practices Habré had perfected. Also, as noted, Déby was personally implicated in Habré's crimes: attention to those would be dangerous for him as well. In 2001 the attorney for a victims' group, Jacqueline Moudeïna, was injured by a hand grenade thrown as she was publicly protesting Chadian elections.

Yet, as discussed in previous chapters, the 1990s was a dynamic decade for international criminal law. The ad hoc tribunals for Yugoslavia (1993) and Rwanda (1994) led to the Rome Statute (1998) and its permanent International Criminal Court (2002). One of the more extreme outcomes of this investment in law as an objective, measurable force in governance (rather than a subjective, contextualized, embedded institutional actor) was an emerging call for "universal jurisdiction" for internationally recognized crimes. Jurisdiction governs the rules under which courts may engage a subject and is a defining notion of judicialism. The first question each court must ask is "May we hear this?" Most written decisions thus begin with explicit recitations of how a court has established its jurisdiction, the gateway question for applications of law and determinations of outcome.

Universal jurisdiction reimagines this essential element of judicial power by suggesting that some crimes, universally acknowledged as criminal, carry jurisdiction in their own DNA. Mary Robinson of the United Nations defined it thus: "The principle of universal jurisdiction is based on the notion that certain crimes are so harmful to international interests that states are entitled—and even obliged—to bring proceedings against the perpetrator, regardless of the location of the crime or the nationality of the perpetrator or victim."[15] The jurisdiction question is therefore not "what is the ambit of the court," but rather "what is the nature of the crime?" Universal jurisdiction expands the particular jurisdiction that courts enjoy, establishing that some state acts are crimes, that is, are beyond the pale of acceptable statecraft or legal forms of fighting (war crimes). Universal jurisdiction imagines, given agreement about the substance of the actions as crimes, that jurisdiction should be established widely in domestic courts and not relegated only to specialized international courts.

There were early forays into expanding universal jurisdiction in domestic law in the 1990s, with Belgium leading the way. The explosion of discussions of the power of universal jurisdiction came later in the decade, in 1998, when Judge Baltasar Garzón of Spain issued an arrest warrant for the Chilean dictator, Augusto Pinochet, who had traveled to the United Kingdom for medical treatment. Garzón requested that the UK extradite Pinochet to Spain to be tried for crimes he had committed as president of Chile from 1973 through 1990. Garzón claimed his court had jurisdiction over Pinochet under universal jurisdiction. The House of Lords ruled in favor of extraditing Pinochet, a decision ultimately overruled by the UK home secretary, due to Pinochet's ill health. Although Spain failed to procure Pinochet, his prosecution and the House of Lord's decision appeared to unlock a political obstacle at home; on his return to Chile, domestic efforts to prosecute him for human rights abuses were revitalized. Pinochet died in 2006 while under house arrest, with more than 300 criminal charges against him relating to human rights abuses (as well as financial crimes). Pinochet was a first, successful trial of the capacity of universal jurisdiction to ruin a dictator's quiet retirement.

In 1999, emboldened by the Pinochet affair, Human Rights Watch (HRW), a nongovernmental organization, targeted Habré as a good candidate to bring the norms and practices of universal jurisdiction to Africa. The case against Hissène Habré had all the makings for success, including an active, organized victims' association and a potentially sympathetic, and highly capable, state (Senegal). Working together with Chadian victims and rights activists, Reed Brody of HRW took on the task of bringing Habré to justice: it would occupy him for the next twenty years.

In 2000 Habré's Chadian victims, assisted by HRW, filed complaints against the former dictator in Senegal, Belgium, and Chad. In Senegal the case proceeded to an investigating judge, who issued an indictment against Habré, who was then placed under house arrest. On appeal, however, the case was dismissed on jurisdictional grounds.[16] In 2001 this decision was confirmed by Senegal's highest court, the Cour de Cassation, which ruled that Senegal lacked jurisdiction over Habré because the crimes were not committed in Senegal.[17]

In 2002 under Belgium's expansive universal jurisdiction statute, Belgian magistrate Daniel Fransen visited Chad with an investigative team to collect evidence. In 2005 after a four-year investigation, the Belgian court issued an international arrest warrant against Habré, who was subsequently arrested in Dakar. Ultimately, however, the Dakar Appeals Court found it had no jurisdiction to rule on the extradition request, and Habré was released.

Activating International Law Measures

Meanwhile, beginning in 2001 Human Rights Watch applied to the UN Committee Against Torture (CAT) for recognition of crimes committed in Chad during Habré's rule. In 2006 the CAT released a decision granting the application and recommending that Senegal either prosecute Habré or extradict him.[18]

In 2006, responding to growing international pressures, the African Union leaned on Senegal to deal with Habré, and in 2008 Senegal altered its constitution to permit the retroactive criminal punishment of core crimes (crimes against humanity, genocide, war crimes) with an eye to addressing the lacunae in Senegalese law that had precluded indicting Habré.[19]

In 2008, in response to alterations in Senegalese criminal law admitting universal jurisdiction and thereby making his prosecution possible, Habré brought a complaint before the judicial arm of the Economic Community of West African States (ECOWAS), a regional court that hears cases brought by individuals against states. Habré contested the retroactive application of the new Senegalese recognition of universal jurisdiction, which in principle would violate the legality principle. In 2010 ECOWAS ruled that Habré could not be judged by a Senegalese court but rather that the court must be international in character.[20] Recall that this rationale echoes ideas articulated in the International Court of Justice's *Arrest Warrant Case,* discussed in chapter 1. The ECOWAS decision invited Senegal to construct such a court, an idea that had been under discussion between Senegal and the African Union since 2007. Although the African Union had pronounced in 2007 that Senegal should try Habré "on behalf of Africa," the grandeur of the proclamation had not been followed up with any sort of action in the intervening years.

In 2009 the Habré case became the subject of the first judgment of the newly constituted African Court on Human and Peoples' Rights (ACtHPR).[21]

Discussed further in chapter 5, this is a regional human rights court that serves members of the African Union that have signed the court's protocol, currently with twenty-six member states. In this first case before ACtHPR, one of Habré's former ministers sought on behalf of Habré to protest Senegal's constitutional amendment "authorizing retroactive application of its criminal laws, with a view to trying exclusively and solely Mr. Hissène Habré." There is some irony that the very first human rights matter brought before Africa's newly minted human rights court concerned not the human rights of civilian/ citizen victims of a repressive state apparatus, but rather asserted violations against the presumption of innocence of the authoritarian leader himself. The application was rejected, and the ACtHPR refused to come to Habré's aid.

As the above demonstrates, there was much judicial grandstanding regarding the possible prosecution of Hissène Habré. While the victims had aligned themselves with a powerful ally in HRW and the person of Reed Brody, and were creative, and active, in bringing possible judicial mechanisms to bear, the sum total of their efforts was two decades of mildly inconveniencing an ex-dictator living comfortably in Dakar.

The critical push that changed Habré's comfortable retirement, and set the CAE in motion, was a 2012 decision by the International Court of Justice (ICJ), the court serving the United Nations and addressing disputes between states. Repeated attempts by Belgium to extradite Habré had been rejected by Senegalese courts on procedural grounds, and Belgium had brought a case against Senegal before the ICJ. The 2012 decision found that Senegal was in breach of its duties under the Convention Against Torture,[22] and it must either prosecute or extradite Habré.[23]

In that same year, Abdoulaye Wade, who had served two terms as Senegalese president, attempted to challenge Senegalese and African Union policy regarding term limits by seeking a third term. Wade had been a key player in the protective Senegalese politics that sought both to protect Habré against early prosecution attempts and to use the case as a demonstration of international goodwill. For example, the Senegalese foreign minister served as one of Habré's attorneys. When Wade was defeated in his bid for an illegal third term by Mbacke Sall in April 2012, Habré lost his champion at the head of state. With Sall's election, internal political obstacles preventing Habré's prosecution disappeared and an agreement was signed by Senegal, Chad, and the African Union to create the CAE.[24]

Building the CAE: An Experimental Hybrid

The Chambres Africaines Extraordinaires was a hybrid, experimental tribunal situated in Senegal, applying international legal content and operating under local rules of procedure. Its budget of 8.6 million euros (about US$10 million) was financed by a group including the African Union, the European Union, and Chad, which made the largest contribution.

Hybrid tribunals are institutions where "both the institutional apparatus and the applicable law consist of a blend of the international and the domestic."[25] This type of tribunal has grown in popularity in response to the arguable decline in international ad hoc arrangements.[26] This decline is joined by the contemporary "backlash" against the International Criminal Court.[27] Hybrids promise cheaper and faster justice and are more intimately connected to local practices and actors.[28]

In response to what the donor community perceives as the failures of international criminal justice, primarily that it is expensive and enjoys low local buy-in, several hybrid tribunals have been attempted in the past two decades with varying degrees of success. These include the Special Tribunal for Lebanon, Extraordinary Chambers in the Courts of Cambodia, the Special Court for Sierra Leone, Special Panels and Serious Crimes Unit in East-Timor, and Regulation 64 Panels in the Courts of Kosovo.[29]

The CAE was a particularly blended hybrid, novel in the universe of hybrid tribunals. It remained a local court, staffed almost entirely by local judicial professionals. Doctrinally, it applied international criminal law: chief judges of both the trial and appeals chambers had experience working before international criminal tribunals, although none of the pre-trial judges had any such experience. This blend of local judicial officials and international legal doctrine resulted in some predictable difficulties that included conflicts between local and international practice (which technically should have favored local practice, but did not) and conflicts in legal understandings. These examples are discussed further in the next section.

Before turning to the examples, however, it's necessary to know some specific details regarding how local procedure functions in Senegal, which practices civil, sometimes called inquisitorial, law. As noted, the CAE was constructed to specifically follow Senegalese procedure wherever the statute constructing it was silent. Thus, for most court processes beyond specific practices (like the years of experience the CAE required of its judges), the CAE emulated the course of Senegalese criminal law, which itself is based on the French civil/inquisitorial tradition. As is typical in this tradition, the

CAE was built on a two-stage process: during the first stage, a pre-trial chamber investigated the situation in order to issue an indictment (against certain persons), and during the second stage, the trial chamber heard the prosecution and defense's arguments before producing a judgment (which either side could appeal). In Senegalese procedure, the two stages are whole and separate: the pre-trial investigating judges examine facts related to crimes to produce an indictment of the accused. Contested elements of this investigation are appealed to the pre-trial appeals chamber, which makes a judgment. When pre-trial appeals are decided, the contours of the indictment (including what crimes are charged, and against whom) are set and indictment is sent forward. At the CAE, at the end of the pre-trial stage, the investigating and appeals judges of the pre-trial stage concluded their work definitively, and this part of the CAE dissolved. The indictment moved forward to the second stage, where the work of the pre-trial chamber was examined anew, pressed forward by the prosecutor, and heard by the trial chamber and then appeals chamber judges, but within the contours shaped by the indictment.

The pre-trial investigation judges traveled to Chad (thrice) and France (once) to collect evidence, a procedure known as a *commission rogatoire*. A fourth trip to Chad was requested but had to be canceled, because Chad ceased cooperating when the investigation seemed a threat to Chad's president, Idriss Déby. Appeals were heard and the indictment was sent on to the trial chamber. During the process, Habré's selected attorneys were invited to participate, but refused. Their position was that the CAE was an illegitimate institution conducting a politicized prosecution of Habré.

From this point, the trial progressed to the trial chamber. Of the four judges, three were from Senegal, and the fourth, the president of the court, hailed from Burkina Faso and had spent more than a decade working for the International Criminal Tribunal for Rwanda. Following the Senegalese system, civil parties (that is, victims) participated in the process through representation by counsel; at the CAE, victims appeared in two groups, represented by two different teams of attorneys.

The CAE began its second stage of work, the trial, in July 2015. Habré had to be forced into the courtroom, carried bodily in the arms of a security agent. This spectacle caused several local attorneys present to quit the courtroom in protest: trials in absentia are permissible under Senegalese procedure, so some felt that the enforcement of a defendant's presence in the courtroom was itself a violation of the defendant's rights. At the opening of the trial, Habré's attorneys refused to address the court, as their position was that they rejected the CAE's legitimacy to try Habré. Apprised of this beforehand, the trial chamber judges had worked with the Dakar bar on a list of names of local attorneys who might be appointed by the CAE to represent the client. Thus, the opening of the trial against Habré in July 2015 ended in a forty-five-day recess to allow the court-appointed attorneys to review materials.

After the recess, the trial re-opened in September 2015 and ran until February 2016. Witness testimony was heard between September and December, and final arguments were made in February.[30] The judges heard ninety-three fact witnesses. Testimony followed a timeline of persecution of ethnic groups over time, recounting the history of Habré's reign through targeted attacks on certain populations. As regards the dictator's targeting of Arabs and foreigners, some who testified indicated, this was not driven by particularized ethnic animus so much as by an imagined support of political opposition by these persons. The CAE also heard expert witness testimony relating to the political situation in Chad and the death rate in Habré-era jails.

Perhaps the most shocking testimony, or certainly the most unexpected, came from a victim participant who was speaking as a witness. While testifying about sexual violence in the desert army camp of Oudi-Doum, Khadija Hassan Zidane made an allegation that she had not voiced before trial: she testified that Habré had personally raped her four times at the presidential palace before she was sent to the camp.[31] Kaltouma Deffala, another witness testifying to rape in the army camp, verified that Zidane had told her about Habré's rape when she arrived at the camp.

The rape allegation brought many of the procedural discomforts—local practitioners might call them anomalies—of the particularities of the hybrid tribunal to the fore. For example, victims testifying as witnesses were allowed to sit in the galley and watch the trial, where normally one would keep testifying witnesses out of the public trial, to be sure not to influence their testimony. The court-appointed defense claimed that the president of the court had instigated the witness's testimony, because he had pressured her several times to "tell all she knew." In other words, the court-appointed defense felt all this combined to create a set-up and a stark violation of the defendant's rights.

On the other hand, sexual violence remains the most difficult atrocity crime to prosecute for many reasons that begin with the difficulties faced by victims in publicly discussing these acts. Experience shows that facts about sexual violence surface later and often less conclusively than facts about other crimes. In other words, there are many legitimate reasons outside of entrapment that dictate why the witness might have chosen to relate this particular crime only in this particular context.

The judgment was pronounced May 30, 2016. Habré was found guilty of personally, and as a member of a joint criminal enterprise (discussed below), committing crimes against humanity, torture, and war crimes. He was also found personally guilty of raping Khadija Hassan Zidane. In its judgment, the trial chamber found Zidane's testimony credible and, citing international criminal case law saying that corroborating evidence for rape is not necessary, determined that Habré bore personal guilt for rape.

The April 27, 2017, appeals judgment reversed only Habré's personal rape conviction, leaving other legal "requalifications" (this term to be discussed below) made by the trial court intact. The Appeals Chamber judgment upheld the life sentence, reaffirming the trial court's legal findings with respect to all crimes except its conclusion that Habré had personally raped Khadja Hassan Zidane: this charge it overturned on procedural grounds, finding that charging Habré with direct commission of rape was an improper requalification of the charges.

Learning International Criminal Law on the Job

In the following I discuss the type of on-the-job learning in international criminal law that judicial officials associated with the CAE had to undergo in order to take on this case in international criminal law. This is not meant to be a critique of the CAE judges and lawyers, who are serious and very capable professionals. Moreover, on-the-job learning and training are central to the way any professional perfects a craft, and the law is no different. Rather, I wish to consider the difficulties and legal gaps that judicial officials at the CAE faced, and all very much alone. Often, perplexing professional novelties are the topic of professional chatter and development. For the CAE professionals, however, working for this singular tribunal meant little or no disciplinary chatter or comfortable professional setting in which to reflect and seek assistance.

The first Senegalese judicial officials to touch what was to become the case against Habré were the pre-trial investigating judges. There were four working judges and two alternates, all but one of them men. All were experienced Senegalese judges (the CAE statute mandated at least ten years' experience to serve), but none had any particular international criminal law expertise.

In a heated political international justice climate pitting African against western expertise (as discussed in earlier chapters), and determined to ensure the CAE would be, and would be perceived to be, an African-run institution, the investigating judges elected not to seek external assistance. Whereas the prosecutor's office and eventual trial and appeals chambers employed several legal assistants with years of experience working in international criminal tribunals in The Hague and Arusha, the pre-trial investigating judges opted not to.

Instead, in order to prepare themselves to apply international criminal doctrine, the judges used the three months following their appointment (while they awaited specific instructions from the prosecution—a normal Senegalese procedure) to read widely in international criminal law judgments. The judges read up on which crimes are recognized, and how they are constituted as international criminal law. They also researched how liability is established between defendants and crimes. Definitions of commission—how crime is "done"—can become more problematic because different international criminal justice institutions approach this subject distinctly and because the doctrines themselves are often insufficiently formulated (see discussion of *Bemba* case in chapter 1).

The task the pre-trial investigating judges set themselves was therefore quite difficult. All international criminal courts face the question of how to assign guilt to those who have not directly perpetrated crime (those "without blood on their hands"). Two main forms of responsibility are charged: either command responsibility (where one stands above the bloody hands in a hierarchy) or "co-perpetration" (when one is understood to have acted jointly with the bloodied hands). The doctrines of commission are complex, changing, and contested in international criminal jurisprudence. Regarding co-perpetration, two main rival approaches have been developed through international criminal law: "joint criminal enterprise" co-perpetration, developed by the International Criminal Tribunal for the former Yugoslavia (ICTY), and "control of the crime" co-perpetration, developed by the ICC.[32] Another way to say this is that joint criminal enterprise is so strongly contested that the ICC has refused to recognize it.

Here, the investigating judges were walking into a hornet's nest of doctrinal fragmentation. Moreover, problems with the doctrines are not simply instances of different tribunals developing different examples or applications, but more deeply related to the legitimacy and acceptable application of those doctrines themselves. This was essentially the defining issue in the 2018 *Bemba* acquittal at the ICC (discussed in the first chapter). *Bemba* hadn't been decided at the time that the pre-trial investigating judges sat down to familiarize themselves with international criminal law, but the doctrine of joint criminal enterprise (JCE) emergent from the ICTY's case law was already ten years old. It was routinely referred to as "just convict everybody." At the

ICTY, JCE was the silver bullet used by the prosecution to convict whom-ever it put in its sites.[33] The CAE, beginning with the pre-trial investigative judges, did not engage the international criminal law debate regarding how to adjudicate co-perpetration, resting its juridical analysis largely in the ICTY's established jurisprudence.

Joint criminal enterprise was a valid international legal doctrine to apply, certainly. But it would arguably need to have been joined by the command theory, which is the ICC's version of how to ensnare guilty actors without blood on their hands, and arguably more applicable because the ICC is a permanent international court and Senegal is a member, whereas the ICTY was an ad hoc institution adjudicating events on the territory of the former Yugoslavia. Moreover, JCE should be considered with a gimlet eye, because the doctrine can violate key rights of the defendant recognized under domes-tic criminal law. Joint criminal enterprise at its broadest, as it was applied in 2013 when the pre-trial investigating judges studied it, could permit a court to convict a defendant who is *aware of foreseeable crimes* as guilty of those crimes should they come to pass. It is a problematically wide net of culpability that has been significantly walked back by the ICTY.[34]

The pre-trial investigating judges indicted Habré for war crimes, crimes against humanity, and torture under, inter alia, JCE as the mode of com-mission. The indictment took a somewhat "belt and braces" approach to the question of how Habré "did" his crimes, charging him under joint crimi-nal enterprise, command responsibility, and direct commission. For Habré's court-appointed lawyers, however, only direct commission was familiar, and in the forty-five days that they were granted to gain fluency in hundreds of documents collected in two years of investigations, these attorneys did not enjoy the luxury of reading deeply into international criminal law to under-stand its doctrinal singularity. Early arguments put forth by Habré's court-appointed lawyers focused on questions of Habré's knowledge, intent, and participation; the lawyers sought to distinguish the acts of Habré's subordi-nates from Habré himself. In mounting their defense, the lawyers focused on evidence connected to Habré's personal culpability, that is, evidence tying the former dictator particularly to the crimes, thus discounting the theory of commission of joint criminal enterprise that could find Habré guilty of crimes foreseeable from actions he was taking. It is foreseeable, for example, that overcrowding in suffocating conditions such as at the *la piscine* prison would result in death. DDS agents put prisoners in *la piscine*, which Habré knew. Under joint criminal enterprise, it is not necessary to show that Habré directly ordered prisoners be sent to the prison (though, in fact, in some cases such orders do exist) in order to find him culpable of deaths suffered in the "criminal enterprise" that was running the prison. Habré's appointed lawyers were informed of the nearly infinite breadth of joint criminal enterprise under international criminal law as a professional courtesy by counsel for the victims.

As discussed above, the "belt and braces" approach in the indictment also complicated questions regarding Habré's culpability for sexual violence. Crimes involving sexual violence formed part of the initial indictment. The investigating judges found instances of sexual violence in testimonies of victims of Habré's regime and characterized this violence in the indictment as "torture." In the indictment, these charges were made against agents under Habré's control, and Habré's culpability was assessed under the international law norms of command responsibility and joint criminal enterprise.

As the Habré trial progressed, a group of American law professors filed an amicus curiae brief with the CAE urging the court to qualify evidence of sexual violence beyond the proposed "torture" charge. They urged the CAE to requalify the ways in which sexual violence was defined as criminal in the judgment and to find these acts in violation of customary international law. In its May 2016 judgment, the trial chamber convicted Habré of rape and sexual slavery as crimes against humanity and torture. The trial chamber found Habré guilty of these crimes in two ways: first, as a senior official who ordered or was aware of the crimes, and second, as a direct perpetrator (it was this direct perpetration that was overturned on appeal).

The question of how much "requalification" is permitted regarding crimes charged can be a tricky procedural question. On one level, requalification is an adjustment of legal argumentation made around facts as stated in the indictment that should be proved at trial. On the other hand, requalification can change the nature of facts, making less significant charges more significant. In the appeal judgment, the judges found that under Senegalese procedure, because charges are fixed at the end of the investigative phase prior to trial, facts may be requalified as to their legal definition, but no new facts may be added, and the testimony of Zidane regarding Hissène Habré's alleged rape constituted an impermissible new fact.

These examples highlight the problematic application of complex, uncertain international criminal law doctrine in a national procedural environment developed to fully protect defendants' rights. They also raise rule-of-law questions because law, while political in its formulation, should be apolitical in its application.

Conclusion

The Chambres Africaines Extraordinaires has been characterized as a "milestone for justice in Africa."[35] After successfully avoiding prosecution for more than two decades, Habré faced justice before an African court. This court, a cooperative effort supported by western governments, the African Union, Chad, and Senegal, harnessed local expertise and international criminal legal content to complete its work and reach judgment. Thus, for some observers the CAE's capacity to put Habré on trial and convict him for atrocities committed during his reign represents a seminal African example of the "revolution" of human rights in the twentieth-first century, where the recognition of core human rights trumps political might.[36]

Although charged with trying those "most responsible" for the commission of atrocities in Chad, the CAE was, for example, unable to try five other individuals named with Habré,[37] and was nearly dismantled when it attempted to explore questions that might have implicated Habré's successor, Idriss Déby. For his part, Déby, at one time a central supporter of the CAE, having initially signed a cooperation agreement and providing the largest tranche of the CAE's financing, came to actively undermine the court's investigations. In other words, instead of representing a challenge to sovereign impunity, the CAE arguably reified the capacity of the sovereign to define the content of justice, as demonstrated by the tribunal's incapacity to indict or try any defendants whose trial was not sanctioned by Chad's president.

For some observers, Habré, and his behavior, is best understood in terms of *chef de guerre*, a "strong leader." They would argue that Habré's repressive state, designed to protect against Libyan aggression, is the reason that Chad still is a state. Moreover, Habré hardly acted alone: he was received by French and American presidents who also financed his regime and sponsored his military initiatives. Thus, Habré's politics, adjudicated by the CAE as "criminal," might otherwise be understood as "ruthless."[38] Another way to ask the question would be to consider how different Habré's leadership was from that of his successor, Déby. Once Habré's right-hand man, Déby borrowed many of Habré's tactics, and even some of his staff, to pursue similar statecraft for thirty years of repressive rule.

In the Habré trial, the critical question regarding how international criminal law might differentiate "ruthless" state behavior from criminal state behavior is left unanswered. Instead, although international criminal law is employed to target the humanitarian law violating practices of the repressive state, the CAE seems only to have captured Hissène Habré, the man.

It was able to do so precisely because Habré had become a private citizen: although once powerful, three decades of spending the spoils looted from Chad's treasury had rendered Habré, in the words of one local attorney, "inconsequentia." Before the trial, as has been noted, the ex-dictator lived quietly between two homes in two posh Dakar neighborhoods as a private citizen and was primarily known as a family man who had contributed generously to local Muslim organizations.[39] With minimal political salience, Habré made a relatively easy target. His prosecution represents a nearly costless way for the African Union, Chad, and Senegal to appease persistent calls for justice from human rights groups and other interested international parties. Moreover, at a time when the African Union is challenging powerful global powers over its relationship with the International Criminal Court, the specter of a trial responding to concerns regarding African recognition of atrocity crimes and rejecting impunity is politically useful. From this perspective, Habré represented low-hanging fruit tried at little cost with potentially significant gain.

The CAE showcases both the possibilities and prevarications inherent in tasking local judicial systems to address state-sponsored atrocity crimes. On the one hand, the CAE worked without violent incident (no dead witnesses, no social unrest) and showcased the professionalism of the Senegalese judicial apparatus. On the other hand, the CAE was only able to convict Habré once he was rendered powerless and was unable to impact the current repressive political landscape in Chad. In producing a foregone conclusion without effecting other significant social change, the CAE highlights an inability of international criminal law to "speak truth to" those currently enjoying power, a central rule-of-law tenet.

FOUR

Courts for Peace:
The Proposed Hybrid Court
for South Sudan

South Sudan became the world's newest state in 2011. The new state did not have long to celebrate; by December 2013 a brutal civil war had broken out, as the president (Salva Kiir) and vice president (Riek Machar), each representing disparate coalitions, abandoned their implicit agreement to cooperate and cohabitate. This war has claimed an estimated 400,000 casualties and displaced four million people.[1] Sixty percent of South Sudanese are extremely food insecure, meaning that famine looms ever-threatening.

Over the lifetime of the conflict, several cease-fires and peace accords have been negotiated (and broken). In 2015 the Agreement on the Resolution of Conflict in South Sudan (ARCSS) was signed between Kiir's and Machar's parties; by 2016 Machar had fled the country and violence had reignited. In September 2018 a "revised" peace accord (R-ARCSS) was signed, this time by Kiir, Machar, and three other parties, reflecting the growing complexity and fragmentation of power in the country.[2] Although the circumstances of the R-ARCSS did not bode well for peace, as of this writing, the peace is holding,[3] signaling at least the possibility of mitigating the misery of South Sudan's population, if not ensuring stable or otherwise effective, transparent, or liberal governance.

We visit South Sudan in this chapter because the peace sought for that country is explicitly built on transitional justice practices, which in South Sudan's case call both for a truth commission and a hybrid tribunal. The Hybrid Court for South Sudan (HCSS) should have primacy over South Sudan's judicial system, be completely independent from South Sudan's judiciary, and have jurisdiction over atrocity crimes committed from December 15, 2013, through the end of the "transition period," a period that still is undefined.

Tribunals are disruptive to peace because it can be difficult to bring warring powers to the table when they (correctly) believe they risk trial, and eventually jail, with the cessation of hostilities. Early studies of transitional justice practices focused almost exclusively on what was understood to be the "peace versus justice" dilemma; how do you convince implicated parties to work for peace when peace means not simply cooperation, but potentially a very bad outcome for the leaders involved? This credible problem is the rationale behind Article 16 of the International Criminal Court (ICC), which gives the UN Security Council (whose mandate is global peace) veto power over the ICC investigations or prosecutions.[4] The collective value of peace can in some cases override the individualization of justice.

Despite these obstacles, both the 2015 and the 2018 South Sudanese peace accords call for trials, even though it seems likely that all signatories to the peace accords would risk investigation and prosecution for crimes against humanity and war crimes under any objective, even-handed procedure in the event hybrid tribunals were put in place. Experts and observers disagree about the utility of trials and doubt that they will take place in any event.[5] This chapter thus explores why the call for hybrid tribunals was included in the peace accords, given the practical and political obstacles that impede them.

The chapter proceeds in two parts. First, it lays out the rationale for transitional justice even (and especially) in relation to fragile states. This is an expanded consideration of ideas the book has visited before regarding the power of law and legal processes to shape domestic institutions and social narratives and expectations. Then it examines South Sudan to consider why the parties to the peace, both internally and externally, keep pressing for a tribunal that most of them doubt will ever come to pass.

Transitional Justice: Employing Courts to Facilitate Peace

We have discussed before (introduction, chapter 1) how law is an unlikely and imperfect response to violence aimed at the most vulnerable populations. Yet since the end of the Cold War, the theory that rule-of-law processes ensure and sustain peace has fueled several ad hoc, as well as hybrid, tribunals. It also underwrites transitional justice. Judicial accountability for violations of core human rights (genocide, war crimes, crimes against humanity) is a key principle of transitional justice, a normative and theoretical discourse rooted in law and political science that highlights the necessity of acknowledging past violence in order to build a secure future.[6]

Transitional justice formally commenced in the 1980s in Latin America, as countries "transitioned" away from authoritarian regimes. Beginning in the 1990s, a burgeoning international criminal law practice sought to address the worst infractions of authoritarian states by putting individuals on trial for violations of core human rights. International criminal law thus joined constitutional consultation, human rights articulation, and civil society support in the arsenal of legal mechanisms to develop good governance in states understood to be moving from autocracy to democracy.

Transitional justice began as a process designed to address the particularities of post-authoritarian countries, based on the specificity of that country's challenges. This is reflected in the seminal book in the field, Ruti Teitel's *Transitional Justice* (1999). There, Teitel argues that the justice that is applied in transition will be particular and temporary. Thus, transitional justice could take the form of "lustration" (rejecting politicians active during authoritarianism for a period of time following transition), truth commissions, or amnesties. The central idea is that the "justice" applied need not meet the standards of long-term fairness, but rather can be crafted to the particulars of the problem being met and overcome. It would surely violate most notions of human rights to impose lustration laws disallowing a certain group to participate politically. During transition, however, lustration can allow new ideas to surface (although it is usually imagined as a temporary, not permanent, measure).

Simultaneously, in the 1990s, ad hoc tribunals for Yugoslavia (1993) and Rwanda (1994) (see chapter 2, this volume) were set up under the UN Security Council's Article VII Peace and Security powers. More tribunals followed, both international and hybrid (where internationals and locals share the work and collaborate on the structure and legal content; see chapter 3, this volume). These tribunals, practicing and expanding international criminal law, could only be weakened by an acknowledgment that justice might be particular or contextual (that is, the sort of justice imagined by early transitional justice scholars). The rule of law requires objectivity, predictability, and neutrality; contingent treatment challenges rule-of-law ideology. Gradually it was tribunals, constructed under the banner of transitional justice, that emerged as central transitional justice mechanisms. This in turn changed the imagined institutional constraints of the field.[7] Presently, the legal rule-of-law philosophy countermanding impunity is central; law is objective and must be evenly applied. This has led to situations like that in Colombia where decades of war were addressed by a 2016 peace deal. This deal imagined the possibility of amnesties and alternate forms of punishment. In response, the International Criminal Court has threatened not to recognize such amnesties, as it argues they may violate its mandate to fight impunity.[8]

The field of transitional justice has been significantly retrenching in the past several years.[9] This is because—in spite of early optimism regarding the socially constitutive power of justice mechanisms—as time passes it is grow- ing ever more possible to assess the dispiriting products of transitional justice adjudications in post-conflict countries around the globe. This is particularly true as regards peace; from Bosnia to Rwanda to Lebanon, many countries that have undergone international judicial interventions have not seen transi- tions away from the dangerous politics or ideologies that led to violence, and the peace that exists in those countries is generally enforced through forms of autocratic or patrimonial power, and not the rule-of-law governance that is the aim of transitional justice processes.[10] This lesson is central to a discussion of the inclusion of a hybrid tribunal in South Sudan's peace accord.

One of the assumptions underwriting the use of legal mechanisms to achieve transitional justice is that the exportation of rule-of-law processes can function as a sort of democratic "terraforming." Terraforming is a hypotheti- cal process, popular in science fiction, that transforms a moon or other planet into something Earth-like and habitable. The democratic terraforming tran- sitional justice imagines is the use of law to make state institutions ready for liberal governance. Democratic terraforming is designed to bring norms of universal, individual-based rights inside of countries.[11] Rule-of-law democ- racies have enjoyed several uninterrupted decades of economic and cultural preeminence, and rule-of-law norms, particularly as regards human rights, are credited with ensuring these countries' improvement-oriented relationships between government and the citizenry. Thus, since rule of law is understood as the seed of western liberalism and good governance, law and norms have also functioned as the proposed panacea for the rehabilitation of authoritarian states.

In her popular 2011 book, *The Justice Cascade*, Kathryn Sikkink argued that there is a historical trend moving toward holding leaders accountable for human rights abuses and violence. Sikkink presents evidence of this trend to claim a sort of renaissance for accountability in governance, a baseline of expectation for what good governance is, and an insistence on rights-based behavior by those in leadership positions, as well as transparent practice for institutions. We can understand Sikkink's book as a high point of zeal for transitional justice. In the decade since its publication, the setbacks visited in this book's first few chapters, in conjunction with other events like rising populism and anti-democratic movements in western states, have challenged Sikkink's rosy "end of history" assessment.[12]

Transitional Justice for Fragile States

Transitional justice imagines law as an objective actor that enables conversations outside of the purely political. Yet applications of law, particularly as regards narrative constructions of historical justice/injustice, are politically fraught and can themselves exacerbate, rather than quell, violence. Law and legal processes are necessarily contested sites, where interest and interpretation vie for preeminence. In the wake of violence, the contestation inherent in legal process can often involve narratives of "collective guilt," the responsibility of peoples for the crimes committed arguably "in their name." International criminal law, by individualizing justice, asserts that it would curb this urge, which it labels damaging. Starting with the International Military Tribunal (IMT) at Nuremberg, selected Nazis were tried with the articulated goal of avoiding the collective guilt of all German peoples. Yet collective responsibility stubbornly adheres nonetheless, from Allied propaganda posters in occupied Germany showing horrific images from death camps and informing Germans "these atrocities, your fault!" through to present-day adjudications, such as the guilty plea presented by Bosnian Serb co-president Biljana Plavsic to the International Criminal Tribunal for the former Yugoslavia in 2003, stating that she had chosen to cooperate with the court "to spare [the Serb] people."

Many were, and remain, skeptical of the possibility of rights protections beyond and outside of the state.[13] This may be part of the growing popularity of hybrid tribunals, internationally funded local courts that apply internationally developed doctrine and standards via local actors, institutions, and procedures. Hybrid courts come in many models (discussed in chapter 3). Hybrids promise cheaper and faster justice and are more intimately connected to local practices and actors.[14] Hybrid tribunals appear to be growing in popularity as judicial elements of a transitional justice, post-conflict strategy in response to the arguable decline in international ad hoc arrangements. This decline is joined by the contemporary "pushback" against the ICC discussed in chapter 1.

When war broke out in South Sudan in 2013, stymied peace actors reached hopefully for legal mechanisms to address or deter atrocity crimes. Less than one year into South Sudan's civil war, the African Union (AU) issued a 315-page report calling for, among other things, the construction of a hybrid tribunal in order to hear abuses committed by the government and other actors.[15] The AU found "the importance of accountability [to be] a constant refrain" across South Sudan[16] and endorsed the creation of a hybrid tribunal for South Sudan as both an essential element of a peaceful resolution to the conflict as well as a necessary building block for the transitional state. It is not clear how or where the AU deduced this "constant refrain"; NGO investigators working with South Sudanese populations report that peace and food security are the topics that unite the population.[17]

The inclusion of the HCSS in the terms of the peace is designed to help build a liberal democracy in South Sudan by addressing the past and building the future: this is the design of transitional justice. Real peace would be unattainable, the theory goes, without the HCSS involvement. In the next section, I consider the specific elements of the lived situation in South Sudan to highlight the question this chapter investigates: whose theories are driving the hybrid tribunal for South Sudan, and how will they be operationalized in the institution and its practice?

Regulating Violence in the World's Newest State

Of the many sad ironies that abound in relation to South Sudan, one that stings any proponent of human rights is that at present the country's rival and oftentimes foe—Sudan—stands as one of two guarantors of South Sudan's peace and prosperity. The other is Uganda. Deputizing Sudan and Uganda as peace enablers has the benefit of acknowledging, and engaging, two significant external power players in the internal politics of South Sudan. In terms of stability and rule of law, however, this engagement is more problematic. Sudan has been a rule-of-law pariah for decades under the leadership of Omar Al-Bashir, who is the subject of an ICC arrest warrant (see chapter 1). Al-Bashir was deposed in 2019, tried in Sudan on corruption charges, and sentenced to two years in jail. As of this writing, the provisional Sudanese government has reversed its stance and agreed to honor the ICC's arrest warrant to hand Al-Bashir over to the court in relation to atrocity crimes in Darfur committed in 2005; this will be significant for the ICC if it comes to pass. Nevertheless, the fledgling Sudanese regime has already been implicated in its own atrocities, with the most egregious incident the murder of dozens of protesters in a coordinated military attack in June 2019. As of this writing, a power-sharing agreement between the military government and leaders of the democracy movement in Sudan is in effect. It sets out a three-year transition period that will end in elections, and we can but hope that this sets Sudan on a less authoritarian path. As for Uganda, the authoritarian rule of Yoweri Museveni continues unabated. By most accounts, Museveni has had a hand in all of Africa's most violent conflicts of the past three decades, beginning in Uganda in the 1980s and continuing through what some recognize as the genocide of the Acholi people. Helen Epstein's 2017 book, *Another Fine Mess: America, Uganda, and the War on Terror*, links Museveni, financed by the United States as part of the war on terror, to the personage of Joseph Kony and the depredations of the Lord's Resistance Army, Kagame's crimes against humanity in Rwanda and environs, and ongoing violence in Congo.[18]

By any rubric—death, poverty, internal displacement—South Sudan represents a human rights catastrophe. Thus, the most pressing concern regarding South Sudan's peace is the question of how to make it last. Violence has been reduced, but not quelled completely, since the signing of the peace agreement in September 2018. Reports of mass rapes by government forces in November 2018, for example, brought sanction from a wide coalition including the UN Security Council,[19] but only denial from President Kiir. In July 2019 a report by the Human Rights Division of the United Nations Mission in South Sudan (UNMISS) catalogued thirty attacks on villages and 104 civilian deaths in the period from September 2018 to April 2019.[20] Moreover, it is not clear what role government forces have in those attacks, or put another way, what capability they have to control them.

Peter Beaumont, a journalist for *The Guardian*, counts more than fifty armed opposition groups operational in the country.[21] Not all major groups have signed on to the 2018 revised peace accord, R-ARCSS, ostensibly rejecting its lack of a guarantee of federalism and power sharing. Perhaps most problematically, a March 2019 report, researched by the International Crisis Group's Alan Boswell, argues that the revised peace accord is yet one more example of a commodified peace agreement ("payroll peace"), which ultimately leads to more war.[22] Boswell's argument, discussed in greater detail below, revolves around incentivization of military recruitment under the terms of the peace. Multiple sources report continued military recruitment, by government and opposition forces, in contravention of the peace accords and including child soldiers (which is never permissible under international law) since the signing of the R-ARCSS. Boswell's points are echoed by the UN Commission for South Sudan, which reported in July 2019 that military recruitment is increasing, making a return to war more likely.

On the other hand, and seemingly impossible given all of the above, a September 2019 article in *The Guardian* described attempts by a newly minted South Sudan tourism ministry to bolster safari and wildlife tourism to the country.[23] If peace can hold, there are many possibilities. This tenuous peace depends not only on South Sudan's own leaders, but on commitments and support from surrounding countries and regional organizations, and here the potential for the Hybrid Court for South Sudan is complicated.

Below I tell the story of South Sudan and how the world's newest state, declared in triumph in 2011, quickly dissolved into pitiless civil war within two years of its formation. This story is rooted in conflicts that raged for decades in Sudan before the creation of South Sudan, and the particular story of South Sudan also intersects with the peace efforts exacted by a troika of foreign players (the United States, the United Kingdom, and Norway). The timeline of historical events in South Sudan, including key players, will help situate the reader. The chapter then applies the asserted benefits of transitional justice—and particularly the application of a court to consolidate good governance—against the particular challenges facing South Sudan as identified by regional experts. The text shows how the use of shorthand risks (justice for peace)

Time Line of Recent Sudanese/South Sudanese History

1956   Sudanese independence established.

1962   Civil war begins in the south.

1972   Peace accord signed in Addis Ababa grants self-governance to south.

1978   Oil discovered in Bentiu, South Sudan.

1983   Civil war recommences in South Sudan, now led by John Garang, head of the Sudan People's Liberation Movement (SPLM); brutal war lasts twenty years and claims two million casualties.

2003   Violence begins in Darfur.

2005   Comprehensive Peace Agreement signed between the government of Sudan and the SPLM.

   John Garang killed in helicopter crash and succeeded by Salva Kiir; unlike Garang, Kiir advocates that South Sudan secede from Sudan.

2009   UN refers case concerning Sudan to the International Criminal Court (ICC), resulting in indictment of Sudan's president, Al-Bashir.

2011   In January referendum on independence brought before the people for a vote, as imagined by 2005 peace agreement held in South Sudan; vote is overwhelmingly in favor of independence.

   South Sudan established as a sovereign state.

2013   War breaks out in South Sudan, and political constituencies are divided between Salva Kiir and Riek Machar, president and vice president, respectively.

exacerbated the humanitarian catastrophe suffered in South Sudan, before it examines how building even an inconsequential HCSS may bring eventual governance gains to the country. Finally, the chapter discusses what experts say is actually at issue and what institutional tools are set up to manage problems in the country. Spoiler alert: there is a significant misalignment.

South Sudan: The Conflict and Its Actors

Although South Sudan's five-year civil war exacted a terrifying death and refugee toll, it is not the beginning of its history and cannot be understood in isolation. South Sudan fractured along well-trodden lines that date back to Sudan's independence in 1956. As long ago as the early 1960s, an organized guerilla movement pressed for independence for South Sudan.[24] A peace agreement in 1972 brought violence to an end, until oil was discovered in South Sudan in 1978. Conflict over control of oil and water resources contin-

2014	The African Union (AU) report calls for, among other initiatives, a hybrid court.
2015	Peace accord, Agreement on the Resolution of Conflict in South Sudan (ARCSS), signed, with part V calling for a hybrid court.
	Decree sets up twenty-eight states with new internal boundaries.
2016	In July hostilities flair up with attack on Terrain Hotel.
2017	In February the UN Mission for South Sudan (UNMISS) releases report saying forty top South Sudanese officials should be indicted for atrocity crimes.
	Decree sets up thirty-two states.
2018	Peace accord, Revised Agreement on the Resolution of Conflict in South Sudan (R-ARCSS), signed, keeping hybrid tribunal.
	In November attack in Bentiu; 125 victims of sexual violence treated by Médecins sans Frontières; President Kiir called claims of sexual violence "baseless."
2019	In February UN Human Rights Commission (UNHRC) for South Sudan releases third report.
	In September Vice President Machar returns to Juba.
2020	Decree returns number of internal states to original ten.
2021	UNHRC for South Sudan releases its annual report and renews its mandate for at least one additional year.

ued political tensions between southern leaders, and the Sudan government's consistent undermining of the 1972 peace agreement fueled a resumption of hostilities in 1983,[25] this time led by a rebel group, the Sudan People's Liberation Movement (SPLM) under its leader John Garang. By most accounts, control over South Sudan's oil has fueled conflict in Sudan ever since.

The peace accord signed in 2005 between Sudan and SPLM imagined a unified, democratic Sudan. But John Garang's sudden death in a helicopter crash in 2011 promoted Salva Kiir to SPLM leadership, and Kiir did not share Garang's interest in a unified Sudan. In addition, the six years between the accord signing and Garang's death had not been reassuring as regards Sudan's commitment to the terms of the peace. Thus, while Garang had favored autonomy for the south within a unified Sudan, Kiir was more pro-independence, and the behavior of Sudanese authorities regarding South Sudan's autonomy only encouraged him in this.

The 2005 peace accords called for a referendum after six years regarding whether the south should succeed from Sudan. The referendum was held in 2011 and the population voted overwhelmingly for independence. Salva Kiir became president with Riek Machar as vice president, a power-sharing agreement designed to moderate ethnic discord in a country made up of approximately 12 million people from at least sixty different ethnicities.

South Sudan's war began in the capital, Juba, in December 2013, when fighting broke out between government and opposition forces. The power struggle at the heart of the conflict was between Salva Kiir, the president, a member of the Dinka ethnic group and supported by Museveni's Uganda, and Riek Machar, the vice president, a rebel leader, of the Nuer tribal group, and supported by Al-Bashir's Sudan.

In her 2016 book, *South Sudan: The Untold Story, from Independence to Civil War*, Hilde Frafjord Johnson lays the blame for the ensuing civil war squarely on the shoulders of Kiir and Machar. Johnson was part of the team that orchestrated the 2005 peace agreement, and from 2010 to 2014 she served as the UN's special representative to South Sudan and leader of the UN's mission there. Johnson argues that the civil war is not a result of South Sudan's independence, but rather a leadership struggle within the SPLM.[26] Johnson further argues that no one foresaw the genocidal character of the civil war. Yet violence across Sudan has long pitted ethnic groups against each other and been aimed at soft civilian targets. Valentino Achack Deng's story, retold in *What Is the What* by Dave Eggers (2006), describes violence in the 1980s that foretold the same methods of violence applied in Darfur in the

2000s. An article in *The Economist* from June 2011 described an ineffective South Sudanese leadership pre-independence, catalogued a litany of paramilitary violence directed at civilians, and predicted that an independent South Sudan would be a "pre-failed" state.[27] In April 2019 a diplomat at the South Sudanese embassy in Addis Ababa put the question to me rather more directly: what sort of governance might one expect from a military master, a man who had slept more nights in the bush than he had in a bed?[28] These musings concerned Kiir, but could be equally valid for Machar and many of the other signatories of the R-ARCSS power-sharing agreement. Cooperation, diplomacy, and good governance require skills distinct from success in bush warfare, and leaders in South Sudan have decades of experience in the latter, less in the former.

The UN had already established a mission headquartered in Juba in June 2011 (UNMISS) with about 6,000 troops. It doubled this mission when violence erupted in December 2013; today the mission includes approximately 15,000 troops and 3,000 aid workers. The aim of the mission is protection of civilians and not engagement in military activities. UNMISS is also tasked with assessing breaches of human rights in South Sudan and has, to date, issued nearly twenty reports.[29]

UNMISS has on many occasions presented a military target. In 2014 its camp in Bor was the site of mass murder when an armed group breached the camp, killing more than fifty of the 5,000 people sheltering there. South Sudan's government blamed UNMISS for the killings, saying that shots fired in the air by UNMISS soldiers provoked the armed crowd. The U.S. ambassador to the UN, Samantha Power, reported that rocket launchers were used by the group that breached the UN compound, suggesting a more coordinated attack. The motivation for the attack was related to reported celebrations of opposition military by displaced people living in the camp. As a spokesman for Kiir's government explained, "Anybody who celebrates successful operations being conducted by the rebels against the government . . . is a rebel, and we cannot continue to accommodate rebels inside UNMISS compounds."[30] This is, of course, not a recognized rationale for targeting civilians, which remains absolutely prohibited under international humanitarian law.

In 2015 fighting escalated. In June 2015 UNMISS issued a report stating that "new levels of brutality" were emerging in South Sudan's war, particularly as related to attacks on civilians. In response, the UN Security Council passed a number of resolutions, including a sanctions regime in March 2015 and a travel ban on six high-ranking South Sudanese military chiefs in July

2015. This helped push forward a peace deal (the ARCSS) in August 2015 that imagined power-sharing between Kiir and Machar and contained provisions for several transitional justice mechanisms, among them the HCSS.

The 2015 peace accord officially fell apart in July 2016 when Kiir and Machar's forces reengaged, forcing Machar to flee the country, eventually seeking asylum in South Africa. The fresh violence in South Sudan was catastrophic, particularly as regards sexual violence and murder. In one violent incident that was widely publicized due to the involvement of foreign, including western, aid workers, government soldiers raped, tortured, and murdered people sheltering inside the Terrain Hotel on the outskirts of Juba in July 2016. Government forces of between fifty to 100 soldiers broke into the hotel, where they tortured and raped aid workers and killed a South Sudanese journalist whose ritual forehead scarification identified him as Nuer. UNMISS soldiers were stationed one mile down the road and did not respond to calls for help; the ensuing UN inquiry resulted in the dismissal of the commander.[31]

The South Sudanese army initially disputed responsibility for the Terrain Hotel attack, with a spokesman noting that "everyone is armed and everyone has access to uniforms."[32] Eventually, however, the South Sudanese government prosecuted ten soldiers for their roles in the violence. The soldiers were sentenced by a military court in 2018; the court also ordered reparations. Many commentators greeted this approvingly as a test of Kiir's commitment to adjudicating atrocity crimes. Unfortunately, this appears to be a test the Kiir government is failing. Following the verdict (and mountains of positive press related to the Kiir government prosecuting its own soldiers for atrocities), the file was sent to President Kiir's office, where it disappeared.[33] As of this writing, the file remains missing and thus the appeal is stalled, indefinitely. This means that the monetary reparations ordered for the victims (which, at US$4,000 per victim, was contested by the victims as too low) have not been paid. This is also, so far, a very quiet failure following what had been a very public celebration, that is, the 2018 convictions and judgment that allocated monetary reparations. Moreover, Kiir has the ultimate power to accept or reject judgments of military courts, effectively granting him an executive veto, which he can apply in the future.

In September 2018 a new peace accord was signed and is in place as of this writing. This deal is not only between Kiir and Machar, but now includes a number of other actors. Analysts warn that one danger facing South Sudan is the capacity for leaders to commit their troops in a Balkanized power vacuum.[34] The R-ARCSS maintained the HCSS and other transitional justice mechanisms proposed in the 2015 agreement.

The Hybrid Court for South Sudan

A proposed Hybrid Court for South Sudan constituted part of the peace agreement signed between the parties and guaranteed by the African Union and South Sudan in 2015. One part of the agreement, "Transitional Justice, Accountability, Reconciliation and Healing," called for a commission for truth, reconciliation, and healing, establishment of the HCSS, and a reparations mechanism. The hybrid court, constructed under the auspices of the AU, was specifically mandated to have primacy over South Sudan's national courts, as well as to be completely independent from South Sudan's judiciary. The court's jurisdiction should be atrocity crimes, including other "serious crimes under international law and relevant laws of the Republic of South Sudan including gender-based crimes and sexual violence," committed "from 15 December 2013 through the end of the Transitional Period." The proposed HCSS would have jurisdiction to investigate and award reparations. This distinguishes it from most international criminal courts, which have so far not added reparations to their purview.[35] On December 13, 2017, South Sudan's council of ministers reportedly approved the hybrid tribunal.

The R-ARCSS signed in September 2018 imported this language regarding the HCSS wholesale, with one small, but not insignificant change: where the 2015 ARCSS called for the establishment of a court "to investigate and prosecute individuals bearing the responsibility for violations of international law and/or applicable South Sudanese law," the 2018 language called for a court "to investigate and *where necessary* prosecute individuals bearing the responsibility for violations of international law and/or applicable South Sudanese law."[36] This would seem to suggest that the possibility of prosecutions, never a sure bet with an uncommitted South Sudanese power structure, are further weakened by inserting additional discretion on the part of the proposed court.

The contemporary concern regarding western intervention (or, alternately, an insistence on African ownership) shapes the instrument, which requires that a majority of judges on the court be "from African states other than the Republic of South Sudan."[37] Likewise, all prosecutors and defense counsel "shall be composed of personnel from African states other than the Republic of South Sudan, notwithstanding the right of defendants to select their own defence counsel in addition to, or in place of, the duty personnel of the HCSS."[38] Further staffing is explicitly required to be African.[39] Although a category of "investigator" is named in the document under the heading of personnel, investigators' nationalities are not circumscribed.

The ARCSS also specifies that the HCSS may draw on prior investigatory work. Thus, we should imagine that this category is designed to include work produced by the UN Commission for South Sudan. Set up by the UN Human Rights Council in 2016 with yearly renewals, the commission seems largely aimed at shoring up the proposed, but clearly endangered, HCSS, as it has an explicit mandate to monitor and report on human rights in South Sudan. As of this writing, the commission is still operational. Its work thus represents a legitimized western/international intervention in the imagined tribunal.

In practice and representation, the UN Commission for South Sudan has constructed its work, and value, in the shadow of transitional justice. Commission representatives have discussed the body's value in explicitly transitional justice terms. In statements preceding,[40] and then following,[41] commission investigations in South Sudan, commission representatives have explicitly connected justice and accountability for violence in South Sudan to sustainable peace. In the reports it has produced, the commission has aggressively detailed what it calls a systemic pattern of atrocities. Its March 2018 report (covering 2017) reiterated that "sustainable peace in South Sudan requires that the African Union [and others] address serious international crimes through the yet to be established hybrid court for South Sudan." The report went on, "The grave lack of accountability for gross human rights violations and serious violations of international humanitarian law committed by all parties since 2013 is the foremost factor for the perpetuation of the current conflict." Moreover, the commission estimated that at least forty senior South Sudanese officials should be investigated or indicted for war crimes. The commission is mandated to provide evidence to a future hybrid tribunal that it would assist in setting up and collecting materials to support these future prosecutions.

This naturally raises the question of how impactful and constructive atrocity trials are to achieving peace, something neither the African Union, nor the UN Commission, addresses. Transitional justice insists that the former sustains the latter, constituting a necessary condition; this is part of the accepted policy wisdom of transitional justice, reiterated in documents produced by both the UN and the AU on the topic. Experts on the ground, however, do not necessarily agree. This final section considers their perspectives.

What the Experts Say

In June 2016 the *New York Times* published an op-ed, co-authored by Kiir and Machar, under the headline "South Sudan Needs Truth, Not Trials." The two argued against trials like those imagined by the R-ARCSS and the UN Commission, pushing instead for a "truth commission" and naming the examples of South Africa and Northern Ireland. They confronted the issue of impunity directly. "By taking this path we understand the consequences. We know that it could mean that some South Sudanese guilty of crimes may be included in government, and that they may never face justice in a courtroom." They countered this problem with the examples of South Africa and Northern Ireland, concluding that "there are recent precedents that demonstrate that this route is the most certain guarantee of stability."

Four days after the op-ed ran, Machar disavowed the piece, saying he had not been consulted. Perhaps Machar does not support the wholesale rejection of the HCSS, as expressed in the op-ed, which he and Kiir had signed onto not once, but twice. It makes good sense that Kiir, the most powerful player in South Sudan, would not favor a mechanism capable of adjusting the current power balance, but that Machar, and other opposition leaders, might perhaps be more open to them. Past experience shows that courts can be very enthusiastically endorsed by leaders as regards the prosecution of other peoples' atrocities, but not their own. For those on the losing side of political struggles, however, courts can represent a chance to strike at those in power.

As recently as October 2018, Kiir re-affirmed his support for amnesties (this in spite of his signature on the August 2018 R-ARCSS calling for a hybrid court). And, as discussed above, Kiir has quietly buried even his own regime's military judgment of soldiers' atrocities committed at the Terrain Hotel in Juba 2016.

We might dismiss the disavowed op-ed as representative of the blatant self-interest of leaders disinclined to jeopardize their political fortunes through disruptive court processes. Rejection of courts is not only expressed by the implicated, however. Following the African Union's calls for trials in South Sudan, two leading Africa scholars, Thabo Mbeki and Mahmood Mamdani, published an op-ed in the *New York Times* entitled "Courts Can't End Civil Wars."[42]

A central unresolved question facing South Sudan's leadership has to do with federalism and power sharing. Over the course of South Sudan's war, the organizational structure of the state has changed, moving, for example, from twenty-eight to thirty-two states in 2017. The UN Human Rights Commission (UNHRC) for South Sudan notes that this restructuring was "highly controversial, generating new conflict dynamics and triggering serious human rights violations," and that it "exacerbated historical divisions between ethnic and political factions."[43] This acute observation is no less accurate for being arguably outside the mandate of the commission and distinct from its task of assisting transitional justice mechanisms, including collecting evidence for future prosecutions.

The issue here is that it is not clear how a hybrid court resolves this central challenge. James Okuk, a political scientist in Juba, says the self-interest of South Sudan's leaders, who are focused on individually protecting their hold on power to the exclusion of everything else, typifies leadership styles across groups.[44] We see a gap between how the AU and UN represent accountability of the South Sudanese peoples and the interests and priorities of the armed men that are the power brokers in South Sudan.

Academic expert opinion on South Sudan can be divided into two approaches. The first tackles questions of South Sudan's peace and governance through top-down military-elite patronage. This examines power brokers, military, and paramilitary groups, and the transactional politics of wartime allegiance built around ethnic belonging and payment for services and loyalties. Here experts query how democratic peace can be constructed in a divided, patrimonial South Sudan. Many focus on the R-ARCSS's insistence on a single military as a resolution for South Sudan's divisive politics. The R-ARCSS calls for unification of all armed forces by May 2019, to be housed and trained together. As of this writing, barracks for those soldiers have not yet been built.

Even after the signing of the R-ARCSS, there has been evidence of renewed recruiting by national army and opposition armies. In March 2019 Alan Boswell of the International Crisis Group argued against what he identified as "the perils of payroll peace." Boswell explains how the peace accord is structured to create material incentives for political elites and soldiers to adhere to the agreement. These very incentives, however, create opportunities for players to mobilize for further war. As Boswell explained to the Associated Press, "In South Sudan, manpower is political power. Politicians use peace deals to grow their own armed ranks." Boswell's concern is now echoed by the UN Commission for South Sudan, which is urging parties to the peace to cease army recruitment.

Boswell advocates for "sustained third-party shuttle diplomacy among the regional heads of state who enjoy leverage over South Sudanese politicians." This is complicated by the interests of those state power brokers, which may work against South Sudan's peace. As for the regional institutional power brokers who are tasked with shepherding the R-ARCSS forward, they are stymied by the intransigence of the parties to the agreement and their own weakness. For example, the Intergovernmental Authority on Development (IGAD), an eight-country trade bloc serving the Horn of Africa, is itself the weakest African regional institution. It serves some of the poorest and most violent countries in Africa and has much on its plate, in addition to South Sudan's war. It only recently oversaw the end of war between Ethiopia and Eritrea and is also focused on violence in Kenya and Uganda. IGAD served as a backstop for the 2015 ARCSS and is still involved in the 2018 R-ARCSS, although in a less direct capacity since Sudan and Uganda have stepped in as backers. IGAD representatives are quick to note that they require the backing of the African Union and South Sudan to push forward with R-ARCSS–related initiatives. Meanwhile, the African Union asserts that since IGAD should be driving the process, it must wait for it to act. Representatives from South Sudan likewise insist that while their government is ready to cooperate, other authorities (the African Union and IGAD) must work out between themselves how they are organized.

Other academic experts have published articles pushing back against a top-down, military-ethnic patronage system, arguing that shuttle diplomacy and leverage politics perpetuate, rather than challenge, the brokerage and patronage system. These studies note how the South Sudanese have organized themselves and survived decades of violence. Works by Mark Massoud and Nicki Kindersley point to local, "lived" forms of authority and law that have subsisted through myriad regimes of violence. Kindersley calls this form of organization the "historical geography of local authority."[45]

Focusing on the power of the local builds on themes explored by James C. Scott in *Seeing Like a State*, where he contrasted local "deep" knowledge that permits complexity within management systems with top-down "state authority" that requires predictable systems in order to effectively manage others. Those who adhere to this perspective thus argue that recommendations arising from top-down approaches will be weak or ineffective. Rather, they insist that sustained transitional justice initiatives must necessarily build on the "no-peace-no-war" justice mechanisms that South Sudanese people have built for themselves over many decades. These processes, while flawed, are commonly understood and popularly engaged with, which makes them preferable to processes that privilege continued elite bargaining over power and wealth.

Conclusion

Transitional justice and its central mechanism, international criminal law, enjoys a heady normative basis (no peace without justice) rooted in the received legacy of the International Military Tribunal at Nuremberg. As discussed in previous chapters, the empirics are arguably much more humble. From Bosnia to Rwanda, from Indonesia to the Congo and Uganda, international criminal law has been expensively practiced often with very disappointing results, when what is measured is commitment to rule-of-law liberalism by the government whose reign and work is assisted by the tribunal. Yet when war broke out in South Sudan, both the AU and the UN quickly called specifically for a hybrid court. Given the current zeitgeist regarding the limitations and dangers of tasking judicial institutions with achieving peace among warring constituencies, the repeated calls by both the AU and the UNHRC are perhaps surprising.

This chapter was born of a suspicion that perhaps such calls represented more "humanitarian posturing" than actual problem solving. In this setting, a universalizing commitment to rule-of-law ideals represents an idealistic relation to power and statecraft that is not evidenced by the leaders whose job is to implement these mechanisms. Kiir's September 2018 amnesty is indicative of this lack of will, as is his denial of mass rapes committed by government soldiers in November 2018, three months into the peace. No leader ever hopes to find himself before a war crimes tribunal; commitments to judicial mechanisms always begin as commitments to prosecute the (other) bad guys. These tribunals sometimes (but hardly always) gain institutional legitimacy, or simply wait out the height of government power, in order to realize their rule-of-law mandate and make broad prosecutions possible.

History teaches that tribunals are instituted either in response to external pressure, or with a myopic conviction that the law can be harnessed to identify and punish the conflict's losers. In the case of South Sudan, the R-ARCSS is supported by Uganda and Sudan, neither of which is likely to bring any particular pressure for solutions, based on law, given the travesty that both Sudan and Uganda represent for rule-of-law governance. The UN Commission's erstwhile collection of evidence against South Sudan's leadership seems to promise equal-opportunity pain for South Sudan's leaders, further discouraging their support of a tribunal.

Yet at the same time, good governance is built primarily on recognition of what judicial responses to atrocity crimes entail. The R-ARCSS and the UNHRC have put questions of justice at the center of building a postwar

South Sudanese state. Even as the institutions imagined in that process (centrally, the HCSS) continue not to exist, focus and pressure on the absence of that justice continues. The recognition that atrocities against civilians are an impermissible means of statecraft will always be imperfect in practice. It is the norm behind the imperfect practice that is significant and that can change state practice and citizen expectation. So perhaps this is a final line regarding the HCSS: its backers cannot institute it without local buy-in, and local buy-in is not, and is not likely to be, forthcoming. This means that the HCSS as proposed in the R-ARCSS, organized by teams within the AU, UN, IGAD, and JMEC, may never become a reality. Nonetheless, energies may not have been wasted pushing for an HCSS that will never be.

This chapter has considered the HCSS as an element of South Sudan's peace process, examining what role the HCSS can and should play in South Sudan's peace and reconstruction, asking: how should we understand the HCSS? Answers fall along a spectrum bracketed by desperate political posturing, on the one end, and determined, rights-based state building on the other. The HCSS ticks all those boxes. Regardless, in the "fake it till you make it" school, posturing counts for something, and ideological posturing will be a central element in any transformation of *chefs de guerre* into *chefs d'etat* in South Sudan.

FIVE

The Experimental Jurisprudence
of the East African Court of Justice

Tucked away in northern Tanzania in the shadow of Tanzania's two highest peaks, Kilimanjaro and Meru, the busy, tropical city of Arusha seems an unlikely justice hub. Arusha is the departure point for safaris heading west to the Serengeti and south to Tarangire (a national park famous for its dense concentrations of elephants). This city of two million is traversed by two main roads, creating a lively cacophony of tourists, locals, goods, and buses. Yet Arusha is also, somewhat more quietly, the host of several regional and international courts, the "Geneva of Africa."[1] The UN's International Criminal Tribunal for Rwanda (ICTR), which once operated in the center of Arusha, has moved its archives (referred to as the residual mechanism or MICT) to a hilltop twenty kilometers outside town with stunning views of Kilimanjaro. The African Court on Human and Peoples' Rights, the African Union's human rights court, occupies a complex on the edge of Arusha on the road that leads to the MICT. The East African Court of Justice (EACJ) is housed in a new building complex, financed by Germany, in the center of town (although this is not the court's permanent seat). The proposed international law and human rights court, the African Court of Justice and Human Rights, when it is ultimately constructed, may sit here. Supporting these international judicial structures are the Pan African Lawyers Union (PALU) and the East African Legislative Assembly (EALA). These important, active civil society institutions have engaged with the judicial institutions in town, creating a dynamic and evolving justice scene. All that is missing is a university to study and teach it all, although Japan has been funding the African Institute for International Law, which hopes to begin offering classes in the next few years.[2]

The preceding chapters have told the story of innovative judicial institutions and their capture by sophisticated interests. If law should constitute a response to power, earlier chapters have discussed how legal narratives are themselves an exercise of power and often are neither transparent nor normatively ideal. This final chapter opens a window to recent judicial creativity that is off the radar even for many international law scholars. The chapter examines human rights practice before the EACJ. This is significant because the East African Court of Justice is nominally an economic court tasked with regulating the affairs of the East African community, embodied in a trade treaty between South Sudan, Burundi, Kenya, Uganda, Rwanda, and Tanzania. Human rights questions in Africa are explicitly within the jurisdiction of Africa's regional human rights court, the African Court on Human and Peoples' Rights (ACtHPR). Founded in 2004, the ACtHPR has been gaining traction slowly in countering human rights abuses by states, stymied by a structure that allows states to somewhat invisibly evade the reach of the court. This, as earlier chapters have discussed, is to be predicted: state leaders often want the narrative of rule-of-law respect even while enjoying the freedom to govern as they choose. Meanwhile, the EACJ, against predictions and most odds, has carved out a jurisprudence challenging states on their violations of human rights standards. It has done so even while surviving existential challenges and acting outside of what would appear, at first glance, to be its jurisdiction.

This chapter examines the institutional constraints, challenges, and inventions that have enabled the EACJ, a trade court, to take on human rights claims that elude the ACtHPR, and how the "justice laboratory" of Arusha, itself, may be contributing to that practice.

Human Rights Jurisprudence in the Pantheon of International Criminal Justice

We must begin with a disclaimer: human rights law and international criminal justice are separate fields with separate institutions, separate literatures, and separate studies. The four preceding chapters have all addressed international criminal justice institutions. Building on the international law precedent established at Nuremberg, these courts enjoy a very particular power, which is the power to pass criminal sentences against individuals. The International Criminal Court (ICC), the ICTR, and the Chambres Africaines

Extraordinaires (CAE) all put people in jail. The UN Commission on South Sudan is listing names of rights violators it thinks should go to jail. This was Nuremberg's invention, the idea that international law, the law between states, could be harnessed to try and ultimately punish individuals. Prior to Nuremberg, determining criminality and imprisoning people was a task left to sovereign states.

Human rights courts, on the other hand, don't put people in jail. Neither the ACtHPR nor the EACJ is assigning jail sentences, nor can they. Human rights courts process individuals but take the claims individuals make against states, adjudicate them, and order (that is, recommend) action to states. In this way, they are a kind of inverse to international criminal justice, which imagines individual transgressions, made in the name of the state or its interests. Human rights claims are claims by the individual against a government. The vast majority of cases are adjudicated internally before domestic courts; states remain the most active adjudicators, and defenders, of their citizens' rights. Recall that a human rights court's legitimacy is partially bestowed by the understanding that its function is to defend the basic rights of citizens against government abuse. In this way, human rights courts help perfect state realization of the social contract, which is the idea that regime legitimacy depends on the consent of the governed (see discussion in the introduction).

There is no global human rights court; instead, states have made regional agreements to permit individual citizens to challenge their governments in neutral forums outside the state. These courts are "supranational" but not international—their jurisprudential reach is limited to the regions they serve, although their decisions and rationales are often instructive and referenced by other bodies. Regional courts can provide particular constraints on member state regimes, because they can be more immune from pressure than domestic courts may be and are often effective at promoting their agenda through reputational and other pressures.[3]

In this chapter I move away from international criminal law and look at human rights because of the power-interest paradox of human rights courts and what that means in terms of constraints on state power. International criminal justice constrains state power by making those who act on behalf of the state criminally liable for those of their acts that violate international criminal law. Human rights law also seeks to constrain state action, but does so at the level of the state, without individualizing wrongdoing. Regardless, it is still a constraint on state action and, in this way, can be expected to be resisted by state actors. One central element of rule-of-law liberalism is the capacity of law to bind power, even and especially the power of the state actors that create, apply, and enforce it. Because human rights courts are external to the state, they can also be ignored or otherwise challenged. This means supranational courts are squeezed between competing pressures. On the one hand, their legitimacy resides in their willingness to challenge state practice that violates human rights. On the other hand, if they mount a challenge a state is unwilling to heed, they risk states withdrawing from their jurisdiction. The proverbial rock and a hard place for human rights courts is the tricky balance they must strike as they serve the states that have constructed them.[4]

African regional institutions have a rather mixed record when it comes to institutional constraints on state sovereign power. There are several regional organizations that are served by courts, and some of these courts enjoy an explicit human rights jurisdiction. The most celebrated African regional court is the judicial arm of the Economic Community of West African States (ECOWAS), as noted in chapter 3. ECOWAS has built a steady body of enforceable jurisprudence. At the other end of the extreme is the tribunal constructed under the Southern African Development Community (SADC), which closed down shortly after it was constructed. The SADC story is instructive regarding the challenges and pressures that supranational courts face.

In 1992 ten southern African countries set up SADC with the aim of increasing development and peace through supranational harmonization. Similar to the treaty of the European Union, the founders imagined a tribunal that would enforce the treaty and hear disputes arising under it, as annunciated in a protocol signed in 2000.[5] The protocol made it possible for individuals and states to bring claims against SADC members, provided they had exhausted domestic remedies (this is a typical element of supranational jurisdiction). The court was, nonetheless, a "paper tiger," because under its enforcement provisions in Article 32(5), the heads of state of the ten member countries (known as the "Summit") would be approached in the event of any non-compliance and would take "appropriate action." In practice this meant the executive essentially had final say over the judicial part of the group, effectively rendering the SADC tribunal incapable of challenging internal state rule. As discussed in the introduction, a central benefit of supranational judicial institutions is their capacity to challenge the political actions and interpretations made by state representatives.

The SADC court did not enjoy particular human rights jurisdiction; it was designed primarily to enforce the terms of the SADC treaty, which was a treaty on interstate economic cooperation. Article 4.c of the treaty, however, stated that "SADC and its Member States shall act in accordance with the principles . . . [of] human rights, democracy, and the rule of law."[6] This provision was interpreted by the tribunal as enabling it to hear cases involving individuals' claims against their governments. Between 2005 and the tribunal's closure in 2010, it heard fewer than twenty cases, which fell generally within three categories: employment disputes involving SADC itself; commercial disputes between companies and states; and human rights cases brought by individuals against their governments. In its short existence, all the human rights cases the SADC heard were against one state, Robert Mugabe's Zimbabwe.

The case that brought the tribunal down was in fact the first it decided in 2008: *Campbell* v. *Republic of Zimbabwe*. The issue was the wide-reaching land expropriation undertaken by Mugabe. The complaint was made by a white farmer, Mike Campbell, who refused to sell his farm, was harassed by armed members of the government security forces, and was ultimately forced off his land.[7] Frustrated by inaction within Zimbabwe, Campbell brought his case to SADC, which ruled in his favor, determining that uncompensated expropriation and racial discrimination had both occurred.[8] The SADC tribunal's determination covered not only the Campbell farm but also seventy-eight other white farmers who had faced similar expropriations and were allowed to join the case. The SADC tribunal ordered the state of Zimbabwe, "to protect the possession, occupation and ownership of the lands of the Applicants" and "to pay fair compensation, on or before 30 June 2009" to the applicants whose land had been expropriated.

Zimbabwe did not pay. Over the next three years, the case reappeared before the SADC tribunal three times. Each time, an interim order regarding Zimbabwe's noncompliance was issued and sent to the SADC Summit to determine what measures might be appropriate. Finally, in 2010 the heads of state in the Summit referred the matter to their justice ministers, who set up a commission to investigate whether the SADC tribunal was properly constituted. The answer came back in the affirmative, but the Summit suspended the SADC tribunal indefinitely anyway. In 2014 the SADC tribunal was reconstituted but its capacity to hear individual complaints was removed, rendering it meaningless. The SADC tribunal has remained dormant ever since.

Reactions to the SADC Summit's strong-arming were vocal and aggrieved. Many observers were particularly perplexed that South Africa, with its strong if imperfect commitment to rule of law, would acquiesce to this patently illiberal move made in defense of a notorious autocrat such as Mugabe. Writing at the time, Merran Hulse argued credibly that a combination of politics and self-interest explained the failure of South Africa to defend the SADC tribunal. Hulse argued that Mugabe was a revered "founding father" for throwing off a minority government (as South Africa had done) and also well-regarded for tackling issues of land ownership reform—albeit using violent and illiberal means—and this also resonated in South Africa.[9]

South Africa did not extend the SADC tribunal as the lifeline observers might have expected at the time. The times are changing, however. A 2018 decision by the South African Constitutional Court found that Jacob Zuma's government acted unconstitutionally in closing the SADC tribunal; specifically, the court found the president's actions at the time "invalid, unlawful and irrational."[10] The Constitutional Court also instructed South Africa's president not to rejoin the SADC treaty as long as individuals were prohibited from petitioning to seek redress through the tribunal. This has sparked discussion of whether the SADC tribunal will be meaningfully resurrected, and in what form.[11]

EACJ: Revolutionary Jurisprudence

The SADC tribunal is a cautionary tale that must necessarily inform consideration of the East African Court of Justice (EACJ). Founded in 2001, the EACJ heard its first case in 2005. The court works only four months a year, which is typical of courts across the region, including, for example, the African Court on Human and Peoples' Rights. Now, however, the EACJ is facing a case backlog, which has led the judges to try to amend the budgeting process and add ten days to the work year. The next challenge, according to one judge, is to secure a permanent court, which has been requested.[12]

The EACJ is a trade court and was established to hear cases arising under the East African Community charter, a treaty designed to facilitate trade relations between east African countries. This was traditionally Kenya, Uganda, and Tanzania and was expanded in 2009 to include Burundi and Rwanda and in 2016 South Sudan.

The roots of the East African Community (EAC) go far back, originating in colonial rule. Before the EAC was established, other regional institutions existed, such as the East African High Commission and the East African Common Services Organization. The East African Community treaty (2000) itself recognizes this heritage, opening its preamble with a recitation of regional unification efforts that date back to 1897. Thus, far from being a court that sprang from a treaty in 2000, the EACJ is the descendant of more than 100 years of colonial traditions seeking regional unity and using courts to standardize and unify.[13]

Once the East African Community was set up, the EACJ became an organ designed to interpret the treaty, although the potential for widened jurisdiction, at some future point, was imagined. Article 23 defined the role of the court as "ensur[ing] the adherence to law in the interpretation and application of and compliance with this Treaty" under Article 27(1). Article 27(2) imagined future jurisdiction that might include "original, appellate, human rights and other jurisdiction" though only when partner states had concluded a protocol to operationalize the extended authority. Chapter 8, Articles 23 to 47, describes the EACJ, its judges, and its jurisdiction. The founders did not anticipate that the EACJ would play an active role in regional integration.[14] Thus, in the parts of the treaty expressly describing the EACJ, it is very explicitly not a human rights court.

The area of the treaty that proved critical to establishing the EACJ's human rights jurisprudence appears in Article 6, which generally addresses the "Fundamental Principles of the Community." According to the text, these fundamental principles shall "govern the achievement of the objectives of the Community by the Partner States," including a series of general qualities such as "mutual trust" and "peaceful co-existence and good neighbourliness." A separate section specifies that fundamental principles also include "good governance including adherence to the principles of democracy, the rule of law, accountability, transparency, social justice, equal opportunities, gender equality, as well as the recognition, promotion and protection of human and peoples' rights in accordance with the provisions of the African Charter on Human and Peoples' Rights." Following in the text, Article 7(2) states, "The Partner States undertake to abide by the principles of good governance, including adherence to the principles of democracy, the rule of law, social justice and the maintenance of universally accepted standards of human rights." It is these two articles—Articles 6 and 7—that have provided the basis for the EACJ's human rights jurisprudence.

As noted above, what began as a trickle is emerging as a tsunami: by some estimates 90 percent of the cases now before the EACJ concern human rights violations.[15] But before this came to pass, the EACJ had to survive an SADC tribunal-type challenge. This challenge came from Kenya, in 2006.

Kenyan Strong-Arming: The 2006 Amendments

In 2006 the EACJ issued an interim order in *Anyang' Nyong'o and others* v. *Attorney General of Kenya*.[16] The case concerned Kenyan methods for appointing representatives to the East African Legislative Assembly (EALA). Opposition politicians within Kenya objected to the methods used by the Kenyan National Assembly and brought the case to the EACJ.

The EACJ's interim decision restrained the Kenyan appointees from joining the EALA, holding up its session. Kenya reacted strongly to the EACJ's interim decision and what it found an unacceptable intrusion in domestic affairs. Kenya took three courses of action to push back against the court even as it awaited a final decision on the merits.[17] First, Kenya attempted to suppress the EACJ entirely (as had been done with the SADC tribunal). This was resisted by the other East African Community member states, at the time Tanzania and Uganda, who were unwilling to sacrifice the benefits of regional integration for what was essentially an internal Kenyan political struggle.[18] Second, Kenya began a campaign against Kenyan judges on the EACJ, pushing them to recuse themselves. Finally, Kenya sought to reform the EACJ, successfully pushing through two amendment packages in December 2006 and May 2007. Hotly contested by civil society and other observers, these amendment efforts were successful and succeeded in altering the EACJ in two significant ways, discussed further below.

The EACJ's ruling on the merits of the *Anyang' Nyong'o* case was issued in February 2007. It found against Kenya and ordered Kenya to change its processes of appointing representatives to the EALA. The EACJ concluded its ruling with the following observation regarding sovereignty:

> When the Partner States entered into the Treaty, they embarked on the proverbial journey of a thousand miles which of necessity starts with one step. To reach the desired destination they have to ensure that every subsequent step is directed forward towards that destination and not backwards or away from the destination. There are bound to be hurdles on the way. One such hurdle is balancing individual state sovereignty with integration. While the Treaty upholds the principle of sovereign equality, it must be acknowledged that by the very nature of the objectives they set out to achieve, each Partner State is expected to cede some amount of sovereignty to the Community and its organs albeit in limited areas to enable them to play their role.[19]

By bringing up the question of sovereignty and influence directly in its ruling, the EACJ sought to meet an SADC-style challenge to its jurisdiction and authority. The question of sovereign power underwrote Kenya's argument in the case as well as the methods it used to challenge the EACJ as the case was ongoing. The EACJ did not deny that its existence deprived Kenya of some sovereignty, but instead made an argument for why such a loss of sovereignty was necessary for supranational integration.

Meanwhile, as noted, Kenya had been actively working to influence the EACJ, and succeeded in pushing through two significant amendments. The first amendment added an appeals division that more than doubled the number of judges working on the court. This was designed to dilute the power of the judges then serving, as well as to add an extra layer of judicial conservatism to stymie what was understood as a judicially creative and independent court.[20] The second change to the EACJ set a two-month statute of limitations for bringing a case, a lightening quick turnaround in judicial terms designed to limit the capacity of parties to bring cases before the court.

On its face, the addition of the appeals division was suitably destructive to the tribunal. Not only did it invite "another bite at the apple" for determinations made by the trial chamber, but it also facilitated delay tactics, because now both judgments and interim orders could be appealed. In this way, the appellate division could be used to delay, in some cases repeatedly, the judgment. This was the case in the Uganda "Walk to Work" case, which lasted seven years.[21] Typically, one way to discourage the use of interim order appeals as a delay tactic is to grant costs to parties. Given that the parties here are states, for whom costs do not represent a major obstacle, however, granting costs is not a significant deterrent to appealing interim orders as a method of delay.

It was assumed that packing the EACJ with judges would result in government friendly advocates, but this is not, in fact, what has happened.[22] The appeals jurisdiction has not had the diluting impact that was originally imagined. For example, Kenya appealed the *Anyang' Nyong'o* decision in a series of convoluted actions, challenging both the process and questions regarding financial recompense. Both appeals were rejected by the newly constituted appeals chambers, voicing strong objections to Kenyan tactics and processes.

There is an unlikely argument in favor of the appeals division. According to one EACJ judge, the appeals division has worked out differently from what Kenya intended because of, and not in spite of, the addition of extra personnel and another layer of jurisprudence. It is, of course, true that the appeals division was set up to constrain EACJ judges. Since its construction, however, the division has arguably augmented the decisions, legitimacy, and legal reasoning of EACJ judges, with the net effect of strengthening EACJ judgments. According to that same EACJ judge, the appeals division "helps cool everything down. The first instance judgment is hotly debated, but with the appeals division, issues cool off. The wait gives everyone time to think. And then, once two chambers decide something and agree, it feels like that decision can't be wrong. It's a safety valve."[23] Thus, a mechanism constructed to weaken the

EACJ has ultimately undergirded its legitimacy. The use of appeals to delay continues to challenge the court, but as of this writing eventual determinations have not walked back the court's progressive, state-constraining mandate.[24]

The two-month limitation, on the other hand, does not appear to have a silver lining. Two months is a very short time for an applicant to bring a claim. More restrictively still, the EACJ has interpreted the two-month limitation to accrue from the start of violation. This means that continuing conditions do not override the two-month limitation; if some act that appears to violate the EAC began more than two months ago, the EACJ cannot exercise jurisdiction over it.[25] The EACJ has declined to consider the validity of the two-month rule under its own treaty.[26] This is distinct from other regional courts, like ECOWAS, which allow up to three years to bring a claim.[27]

Constructing a Human Rights Mandate

The EACJ's ground-breaking human rights case was *Katabazi* v. *Uganda*, brought in 2008,[28] two years after the challenges brought by Kenya and passage of amendments to the court discussed above. The case concerned a brazen example of illiberal government action. Twenty-two opposition politicians and their supporters, accused of treason by the Ugandan government, appeared before a Ugandan court. The court ordered fourteen of them to be released from detention. The Ugandan government responded by sending security forces to the court to re-arrest the released applicants, in contravention of the court's order. The applicants applied to Uganda's Constitutional Court, which ruled the government action was unconstitutional. This resulted in no change in status for the applicants, however; they remained in prison. This so far describes a relatively run-of-the-mill set of authoritarian state actions, repeated in many corners of the world.

What happened next shows phenomenal judicial creativity and precision, first on the part of the opposition politicians' (the applicants') lawyers, and then by the court.[29] The applicants brought a case against the secretary general of the East African Community as well as against the attorney general of Uganda. This interesting set of respondents was chosen in order to push jurisdiction of the matter to the EACJ.

The challenge, of course, was to make a legal, that is to say, jurisdictional, connection between the East African Community's mandate and internal state behavior in Uganda. To put it another way, what business of the EACJ's is it when two Ugandan government organs disagree? The EACJ assumed jurisdiction over the case through the creative interpretation of bits of language found in several treaty articles. These included Articles 6(d) and 7(1), which were discussed above, as well as Articles 8, 29, and 71. These later articles contained general language regarding taking steps to achieve treaty objectives.[30] The EACJ determined that these articles were sufficient to give it jurisdiction to consider the claim against the secretary general of the East African Community by the applicants.

Next the court addressed the elephant in the room: Article 27, which explicitly considers that the EACJ's jurisdiction does not presently include human rights, although such jurisdiction might be widened in the future. This would appear to be a major bar. The court, however, reasoned around this jurisdictional hurdle, arguing

> Does this Court have jurisdiction to deal with human rights issues? The quick answer is: No, it does not have. Jurisdiction of this Court is provided by Article 27. . . . It is very clear that jurisdiction with respect to human rights requires a determination of the Council and a conclusion of a Protocol to that effect. Both of those steps have not been taken. It follows, therefore, that this Court may not adjudicate on disputes concerning violation of human rights *per se.*
> However, let us reflect a little bit. . . .

This the court did, running through the articles in the treaty setting out the "objectives" of the community, including cooperation (Article 5[1]), the rule of law, social justice, and promotion of human rights (Articles 6 and 7), and avoidance of measures likely to jeopardize these objectives (Article 8). Based on this interpretation of the East African Community's broadly stated objectives, the court determined that while it could not "assume jurisdiction to adjudicate on human rights disputes" neither would it "abdicate from exercising its jurisdiction of interpretation under Article 27(1) merely because the Reference includes allegation of human rights violation."[31] Thus, rather extraordinarily, the EACJ asserted jurisdiction over Uganda's internal authoritarian exercise of sovereign authority (police and security questions are a bedrock of sovereignty) under the aegis of Uganda's supranational commitment to the East African Community and its rule-of-law, democratic, and human rights foundations. In its own, quite noteworthy, words, the EACJ concluded: "The intervention by the armed security agents of Uganda to prevent the execution of a lawful Court order violated the principle of the rule of law and consequently contravened the Treaty. Abiding by the court decision is the cornerstone of the independence of the judiciary, which is one of the principles of the observation of the rule of law."

It bears recollecting that this bold pronouncement was made following Kenya's attack on the court and in the shadow of the SADC court collapse.

The EACJ's carving out of a "not human rights *per se*" jurisprudence has been quite successful. It has since decided several human rights–related cases and also has made reference to its own capacity to interpret human rights instruments.[32] As of this writing, the majority of applications to the EACJ are related to state violations of rule of law and democratic governance principles.[33] The EACJ's human rights jurisprudence has become so significant that it has attracted the attention of international NGOs. The Open Society Institute, for example, compiled a list of relevant human rights decisions emerging from the EACJ as a tool for legal and human rights professionals.[34]

One interesting element of the EACJ's jurisprudence is the success it has had even while a court specifically designated to hear human rights cases sits just down the road. The African Court on Human and Peoples' Rights, instituted in 2004, is the African Union's human rights court. It has jurisdiction over human rights claims, and while it, like the EACJ, does not adjudicate year-round, it is enjoying increasing visibility and productivity.

Thirty countries are members of the ACtHPR. In order for individuals to be able to bring cases, however, member states must sign a protocol, and so far, only nine countries have done so. Moreover, to bring cases to the ACtHPR, one must exhaust local remedies, that is, you must take your case through all possible legal options in your home state before applying to the supranational body for adjudication. This is not unusual: the European Court of Human Rights has the same requirement, and it follows on the hierarchies evidenced in domestic systems, where most claims must move up the ranks and are not allowed simply to spring to the top court.

The EACJ has two advantages over the ACtHPR in this regard: it is not necessary to exhaust local remedies (although the two-month rule means one must make a claim very quickly), and individuals can approach the court without hindrance from any state protocol. To bring cases in other domestic courts, many individuals in African states must wait out a years-long process and may, in the end, be barred from approaching the court due to their state's status regarding the protocol granting an individual or NGO access to the court.

This has led, at the time of this writing, to a surge of claims against the government of Tanzania. An increasingly authoritarian Tanzanian state has been cracking down on journalists and jailing them. Conditions in prisons are terrible. Both of these facts have been at issue in a number of cases before the EACJ.[35]

Attempts have been made to use the EACJ to broaden the ACtHPR's reach. The Democratic Party, a Ugandan political organization, brought suit against the Secretariat of the East African Community and the attorneys general of Uganda, Kenya, Burundi, and Rwanda before the EACJ to compel those countries to approve the protocol necessary for individuals and NGOs to bring cases to the ACtHPR.[36] The EACJ found, and upheld on appeal, that it could not compel countries to send the protocol to ACtHPR. The EACJ did, however, reiterate its capacity to interpret the African Charter on Human and Peoples' Rights, as discussed above.

Can the EACJ Go on This Way?

Reading the EACJ's bold jurisprudence, and considering the problematic governance records of the countries that make up the East African Community, the reader would not be remiss to imagine that the EACJ cannot continue as it has. Not a single East African Community country is convincingly committed to human rights–respecting rule-of-law governance: human rights intransigence in South Sudan (chapter 4), Rwanda (chapter 2), and Kenya (chapter 1) has been addressed in previous chapters. Emerging problems in Tanzania are discussed above, and all are encouraged to read Helen Epstein (2016) on Uganda for a disquieting consideration of Museveni's human rights record. My own discovery of EACJ jurisprudence was colored by dread, as I wondered, could such an inventive, progressive court even survive the gestation period of this book?

My conversations with parties in Arusha quieted some of these concerns, however. My interlocutors noted that since the articulation of human rights capacity before the EACJ, the court's cases have gotten bolder and more self-assured. Answers as to why fell into three categories, covering the EACJ's particular structure, the interests of member countries, and the active role of civil society.

First, it seems that the EACJ's particular structure encourages judicial professionalization and independence. For example, judges, nominated by their home countries and protected by their home judiciary structures, serve one, non-renewable seven-year term. They will return to their original positions at the conclusion of their EACJ term. That there is job security for these judges assists in supporting the atmosphere of professional adjudication at the EACJ.

As one judge said, "Judges see the dynamics that lead to independence. The way cases are structured, even if you wanted to throw a case a certain direction you couldn't, so there is no pressure in court to do this; it would make no sense."[37]

Second, backlash is costly. The trend in regional and international courts is that there is one significant backlash—that is, each court faces an existential moment when its survival is threatened—per institution. The EACJ has faced, and survived, its own. For states to keep resisting the EACJ as an institution has reputational costs. Big cases bring media attention, and this can influence states. Also, there are six member states, and none is particularly patient when others hijack the East African Community to wage their own internal fights. While resistance comes with each case, it is fought on the EACJ's terms, within a jurisprudence the court has already broadly enabled.

Finally, civil society in Arusha and beyond provides a justice architecture that effectively supports progressive jurisprudence. NGOs such as the Pan African Lawyers Union (PALU) and the East African Law Society have made Arusha their home, and they are active in bringing cases, organizing lawyers, and articulating positions to state representatives. In part, these organizations have gathered in Arusha because they are in flight from more repressive regimes: Addis Ababa, home to the African Union, would be a natural home for Pan-African organizations, but years of repressive Ethiopian resistance to human rights organizations forced PALU, for example, out. And certainly, the political situation regarding human rights in Tanzania has devolved over the past few years; the current Tanzania regime employs specific measures designed to curtail opposition, beginning with attacks on journalists as reported by human rights organizations.[38] For the time being at least, a critical mass of legal professionals with progressive human rights law at the center of their professional attention is headquartered in Arusha, and this helps support ambitious courts such as the EACJ.

Conclusion: "A Monster to Devour Us All"

"A monster to devour us all"[39] is how the former Tanzanian president described the SADC tribunal as it took aim at Zimbabwe. Yet as is often the case, one man's monster is someone else's hero. To date, the jurisprudence practiced by the activist, human rights–enabling EACJ appears rather heroic. One difficulty, however, with celebrating progressive law is that we risk being seduced by the outcomes, while ignoring the process. The EACJ's work in addressing authoritarian overreach is creative, exciting, and even hope generating. But had the EACJ stepped as creatively around the East African Community treaty to redistribute property or enumerate political participation or any number of other acts imaginatively related to democracy and human rights, perhaps we would be less sanguine about the institution.

Courts are famously problematically antidemocratic. They are understood to protect against what de Tocqueville termed "the tyranny of the majority," sheltering minorities through the articulation of "rights" when minorities cannot protect those rights through straight democratic voting rules.[40] But these same minority protections are also undemocratic by their very nature, since they assure that minority interests cannot be overcome by majority vote. And if we think of minority rights as synonymous with human rights and good governance, it is only because we lack a fuller story. During the Great Depression, American President Franklin D. Roosevelt fought the U.S. Supreme Court over legislation his administration and Congress had passed in order to save lives and address conditions brought on by the Depression. Roosevelt's social programs were repeatedly overturned by five (out of nine) Supreme Court justices deeply invested in protecting the minority rights of property holders and industrial capitalists. The situation only changed when Roosevelt threatened to "pack" the court, more than doubling the number of Supreme Court justices; this threat convinced one justice to come over to Roosevelt's way of seeing and has gone down in U.S. constitutional history as "the switch in time that saved nine."

Around the globe, supranational courts are under pressure from states underwhelmed by these courts' claims to a higher truth, when that truth challenges state action. Even the world's most celebrated human rights court, the European Court of Human Rights (ECHR), has been stepping back its assertive jurisprudence in the face of state resistance. In areas of the greatest sensitivity to states, such as questions of citizenship and asylum, the ECHR has famously never been a friend to rights seekers but has rather tended to defer to states. This pushback against the "justice cascade" may be simply part of an ebb and flow, which may bring regional courts back into prominence in the years to come. In this sense, however, the EACJ may be particularly endangered by coming late to the party, making bold and progressive judgments at a time when even established courts, serving established rule-of-law democracies, are laying low and waiting for populism to pass.

If the EACJ remains alone, if the ACtHPR does not begin to share more EACJ jurisprudence, then we should expect eventual EACJ failure: SADC's example shows how it can happen. For the cascade to be permanent, citizens in the East African Community countries must begin to normalize the values that the EACJ draws on in claiming its remit; that is, democratic values based on the rule of law and human rights articulated in the East African Community treaty, Article 6(d), as well as the expectation that there is someone "considering" (Article 29) and "investigating" (Article 71(1)) who can and will act when states abdicate their rights responsibilities.

CONCLUSION

Changing How the West
Thinks about Africa

The Swedish artist Nikolaj Cyon created the artwork shown on the book's cover. The map originally appeared in his blog, *The Decolonial Atlas*, in 2014. There he used the name *Alkebu-lan* to describe the continent and noted it was Arabic for "the lands of the Blacks," although this meaning is disputed. He indicated this name is the oldest known name for Africa. His map reflects a mind experiment of what Africa looked like in the mid-nineteenth century, before colonialization.[1] Cyon's map captures the size, complexity, and richness of the African continent and suggests its power and centrality. Europe and the Middle East, rendered nearly without color and lacking detail or description, are easily overlooked beside the splendor of Africa.

Part of the power of Cyon's image comes simply from flipping Africa upside down, a time-honored strategy for reconceptualization.[2] Reconceptualization is also essentially the aim of this book. Mainstream considerations of Africa often relegate it to the periphery or place it in a victim/perpetrator binary, where African countries are tragically victimized by a global marketplace in which they cannot compete, or African countries are staggeringly violent, wastrel, or corrupt. Likewise, many mainstream conceptions of international criminal justice often imagine it in a similar manner: peripheral to "real" power, binarily captured between ideological purity and political incompetence. This book has been written to encourage a closer look at both Africa and international justice, in order to challenge simplistic binaries and encourage critical consideration.

This book has told several stories of international justice in Africa. In each example, interests, often in conflict and often contrary to rule-of-law best practices, have factored prominently. These interests are local and political, which includes the interest of the practitioners, developers, and cheerleaders of international criminal justice. In its first two chapters, the book has catalogued failures celebrated as successes: the International Criminal Court, so caught up in its own institutional survival that it took whatever work it could get and did not ask questions, and the International Criminal Tribunal for Rwanda, put in service to a dictator with his own ties to massive crimes against humanity arguably amounting to a second genocide. The third chapter highlights a tribunal recognized for its outcome but more remarkable for its process, which suggests a standard that might inform future models. The fourth chapter studies the problem of empty ideology, and the fifth chapter visits creative jurisprudence imagined and implemented in local conditions responding to local contingencies.

This book surveys international criminal justice across Africa, but of course, it only samples the surface. From the first international/domestic hybrid tribunal for Sierra Leone that put Charles Taylor on trial to contemporary experiments with "roaming courts" in Congo and Uganda, there are several topics in international criminal justice that we might have considered. In these final paragraphs, I'd like to add two additional international criminal justice mechanisms and practices that fall in the "ones to watch" category: the proposed African Court of Justice and Human Rights, sometimes called "The Malabo Court," because it was created as an amendment to the Malabo Protocol, and the 2019 invocation of the Genocide Convention against Myanmar by The Gambia.

The Malabo Court

In 2014 African states adopted the Malabo Protocol as a regional African alternative to the International Criminal Court (ICC). The Malabo Protocol calls for the creation of an African regional court—the African Court of Justice and Human Rights—that would have jurisdiction over human rights *and* international criminal law matters. Currently Africa, like Europe and the Americas, has a regional human rights court, the African Court on Human and Peoples' Rights (discussed in chapter 5). The only transnational criminal court in existence is the ICC, and it is at work on situations across the African continent. There is no supranational court that shares international criminal law and human rights jurisdiction, and thus the proposed African Court of

Justice and Human Rights would represent a significant global experiment, the first of its kind.

The proposed court is innovative beyond its jurisdictional structure. It significantly expands the crime base established by the Rome Statute, adding environmental crimes, corruption, human trafficking, and several other offenses to the cadre of recognized infractions.[3] The core crimes that constitute the mandate of international criminal law—genocide, crimes against humanity, war crimes, aggression—are to some degree a historical accident. They are the crime base decreed or recognized by the Allied powers and their jurists following World War Two, and subsequently enshrined as international criminal law, and do not include the ideas considered by the International Law Commission following that conflict.[4]

The proposed Malabo court was midwifed by Don Deya, a seminal figure in Pan-African justice and human rights and the head of the Pan African Lawyers Union (PALU), headquartered in Arusha, Tanzania. Deya describes himself as an activist; his interest is strengthening human rights, and he believes Pan-Africanism is the means to this end.[5] Deya recounts the process of constructing the crime base of the Malabo Protocol as a gathering exercise. Recognizing that many activities serve as "enabling crimes" on the road to mass atrocity, Deya mined African Union instruments to put together a broad list of recognized crimes; such a list, by being more inclusive, could also better address and deter atrocity. Critically, the crimes recognized and gathered in this exercise were nearly all noncontroversial, that is, already recognized in African Union instruments. The crime of unconstitutional change of government, for example, has a basis of recognition already in the African Charter,[6] and thus needed to simply be gathered and included as the crime base for the proposed court. His greatest "get" was the inclusion of environmental crimes; here he says he really needed to fight to persuade African Union representatives to include it as a category. His successful strategy included convincing African states that recognition of environmental crimes would prove prescient, and states would be remembered for their boldness.

The proposed court makes another innovative move, this one much less popular among many international justice proponents: it explicitly grants sitting heads of state immunity from prosecution. As previous chapters have shown, challenges related to sovereign immunity are at the heart of much resistance to international justice across Africa. The proposed Malabo court seems to nod to the theory that the sovereign is necessarily out of reach of justice by categorically declaring that sovereigns are immune from prosecution.

For this reason, the Malabo Protocol has been rejected by many proponents of international criminal law as a normatively inadequate justice instrument, although recent scholarship by international criminal justice scholars shows that the Malabo Protocol may be enjoying a heightened interest within this community.[7]

So, what to think about the proposed Malabo Court, thus far ratified by only three countries and years away from existence? In keeping with the themes of this book, I think it is a mistake to write the court off as empty politics, a rhetorical challenge to an unpopular ICC, or as a means for corrupt leaders to shellac their bad deeds. Rather, I believe we should take the phrase "African solutions to African challenges" more seriously and not presume bad faith from the outset. The proposed Malabo Court emerged from years of effort made by active and committed African human rights activists; this should at least give naysayers pause before they condemn the proposed court.

Moreover, as preceding chapters have shown, international efforts to pursue sovereigns and accomplish justice have often netted disastrous results. From dead witnesses in ICC cases to dead opposition politicians in Rwanda to Idriss Déby's thirty-year reign in a Chad now receiving international military support (this time to fight the global war against terrorism, rather than the territorial fight against Gaddafi's Libya), international criminal justice has experienced its own share of failure. Certainly, international criminal justice institutions cannot be said to have all the answers. Given this reality, what harm is there in a more generous approach to creative judicial forms? As chapter 5 shows with regard to the East African Court of Justice, judicial creativity is opening unexpected possibilities for resistance to state authoritarianism.

The Gambia v. *Myanmar* before the International Court of Justice

International criminal justice has had another impact across Africa, and that is in the training of professional adherents. In 2019 The Gambia made a novel use of the Genocide Convention to bring Myanmar before the International Court of Justice (ICJ), the UN's court. The Genocide Convention permits *erga omnes* (Latin for "toward everyone") jurisdiction. The rational is that because genocide harms all of humanity, any state may bring a case against another state where it fears that genocide may be taking place and need not have any particular relation to the case, crime, or state. Before The Gambia's case, the Genocide Convention had only been invoked twice: in relation to the wars of the former Yugoslavia and by countries claiming that their own peoples were the victims. In this case, The Gambia did what no other country has ever done. By bringing a case where it had no personal interest in the outcome, The Gambia's claim realizes the promise of the Genocide Convention, a historical first.

How is it that The Gambia, which until 2016 was ruled by a rights reproaching autocrat, was the first to operationalize a central human rights norm? The answer lies in the global professionalization of international criminal justice. The Gambia's minister of justice is Abubacarr Tambadou. He had weathered The Gambia's authoritarianism outside the country, working for thirteen years—the bulk of his professional life—at the International Criminal Tribunal for Rwanda (ICTR). He then took up his post in a newly democratic The Gambia. In 2017 he took the place of the minister of the interior on a state visit to Bangladesh in an unexpected last-minute personnel switch. Visiting the Rohingya refugee camp—Cox's Bazaar, the largest refugee camp in the world—Tambadou says he was reminded of the cases he had worked on at the ICTR. Tambadou returned from this unplanned trip with a changed purpose, determined to use the tools at his disposal to address this humanitarian catastrophe.

At the December 2019 hearing in The Hague, Tambadou addressed the ICJ on behalf of The Gambia, beginning his presentation this way:

> As Attorney General of the Republic of The Gambia, I stand before you today as Agent in a dispute with the State of Myanmar, but not a conventional one that this Court is accustomed to. I stand before you to awaken the conscience of the world, and to arouse the voice of the international community. In the words of Edmund Burke: "The only thing necessary for the triumph of evil is that good men do nothing." Honourable Judges, every genocide that has occurred in history has had its own causes, unique to its historical and political context. But one thing is certain, genocide does not occur in a vacuum. It does not suddenly spring up or appear overnight out of the blue; it is preceded by a history of suspicion, mistrust, and hateful propaganda that dehumanizes the other, and then crystallizes into a frenzy of mass violence, in which one group seeks the destruction, in whole or in part, of another. But when we dehumanize others, we dehumanize ourselves as human beings. For any genocide to occur, two things must be present: a dehumanization of the other and the indifference of the international community.[8]

In articulating the purpose of the Genocide Convention and The Gambia's "unconventional" role, Tambadou built on recognized and accepted international law and humanitarian law norms and referenced the centuries' long intellectual tradition of human rights on which institutions and treaties are founded.

Representing Myanmar was Aung San Suu Kyi, who was awarded the Nobel Peace Prize in 1991 and has since fallen starkly in international esteem. In making the blanket denials that have become her stock in trade, Suu Kyi appealed to The Gambia, as well as other members of the global south, not to accede to the information gathering of the United Nations and other global powers. She told the court:

> It would not be helpful for the international legal order if the impression takes hold that only resource-rich countries can conduct adequate domestic investigations and prosecutions, and that the domestic justice of countries still striving to cope with the burden of unhappy legacies and present challenges cannot be made good enough. The Gambia will also understand this challenge with which they too are confronted.[9]

While Aung San Suu Kyi made this statement addressing the ICJ, her real audience was nations in the global south. This is essentially a variant of the "Africa for Africans" argument that has been raised against the ICC and in favor of Senegal hosting and controlling the Habré trial. This argument, that abuses by powers of the global north against the global south make all activity within the global north suspect, is not novel or modern.

The Gambia's choice to utilize, and in so doing refurbish and seminally expand, an international humanitarian law norm through its prosecution under the Genocide Convention is interesting and important. Myanmar's violent treatment of its Rohingya minority has been a global topic for decades. When more than half a million Rohingya were driven from Myanmar beginning in 2016, many states and international organizations spoke out against the violence. The ICC has sought creative work-arounds to assert jurisdiction over the case, but without Myanmar's cooperation, it is not clear what will ever come of the ICC's investigation, even if it is legally able to proceed. For its part, Myanmar categorically denies wrongdoing and appears to have successfully bulldozed much evidence of burned villages and mass graves in the past few years, complicating assessment, redress, or repopulation of their lands by the one-time Rohingya inhabitants. The Gambia's prosecution of the case before the ICJ has been met by judicial silence.

The Gambia's expansive application of international law and the development of an extended criminal roster by the African Court of Justice and

Human Rights are just two areas the reader may watch for interesting developments. As the book's title suggests, it is Africa's justice laboratories that merit greater attention and interest, and it is this author's hope that readers will not make this book their last stop on a journey examining institutions in or relating to Africa. The century-old dream to protect the most basic human rights of the world's most vulnerable populations through law is on the brink of political collapse: it will either break, or be transformed, in Africa.

Notes

Introduction

1. Sikkink (2011).

2. For example, when the United States lost the political battle to control the ICC, it began working against the institution's efficacy. It pressured several African states to sign agreements promising not to hand American citizens over to the court. In 2002 the U.S. Congress passed a law dubbed "The Hague Invasion Act" allowing the U.S. to "take all means necessary" to free any member of the U.S. military who might come into ICC custody.

3. Since the amendment was drafted in 2010, more than half of the ICC's member states in Europe have not ratified it; there are only 35 ratifications, from 122 member states, worldwide. See www.coalitionfortheicc.org/explore/icc-crimes/crime -aggression. The crime of aggression was officially added to the Rome Statute in 2018 after it passed the threshold of thirty signatures, but so far no one has been charged under it.

4. In April 2021, as this book was going to press, Déby was killed by rebels in a military operation in northeast Chad. Chad is now ruled by a Transitional Military Council of fifteen generals, headed by Déby's thirty-seven-year-old son. See Alexandre Marc, "The Death of Chadian President Idris Déby Itno Threatens Stability in the Region," April 29, 2021, www.brookings.edu/blog/order-from-chaos/2021/04/ 29/the-death-of-chadian-president-idris-deby-itno-threatens-stability-in-the-region/.

5. In the current atmosphere of populism, discussion increasingly turns to what constitutes a "rule-of-law democracy," where some authors contest the American or western European nations' inclusion in this category. See Abel (2018); Burgorgue-Larsen (2019).

6. Brett and Gissel (2020); Caserta and Cebulak (2018).

7. de Tocqueville (2002).

8. Cover (1995); Wacquant (2009).

9. Shapiro (1981).

10. Primus (1996); Roth (2010); Teubner (2015); Carlson (2018).

11. Mettraux (2008); Karnavas (2007); Robinson (2013); Rohan and Zyberi (2018).

12. See *Prosecutor* v. *Jean-Pierre Bemba Gombo*, ICC-01/05-01/08 A (June 8, 2018).

13. In 2018 the ICC's PreTrial Chamber ruled, 2-1, that the ICC could exercise jurisdiction over the alleged deportation of the Rohingya people from Myanmar to Bangladesh, even though Myanmar is not a member of the ICC (ICC-CPI-20180906-PR1403). As discussed in chapter 1, the ICC has limited jurisdiction, which it can exercise over member states or in situations referred by the UN Security Council. The PreTrial Chamber argued that deportation has two phases, a start and a finish, and in this case the finish occurred in an ICC member state, Bangladesh. This, therefore, made ICC jurisdiction possible. In June 2019 the ICC prosecutor opened an investigation into crimes against the Rohingya, discussed further in the conclusion.

14. Most law is domestic, determined by states. Law outside of states can be international, when evenly available to all countries, or supranational, when applicable to some group of countries, usually based on regional membership in an organization.

15. This is surprising because we assume that states want to control their criminal law docket themselves, in accordance with Max Weber's (2013) infamous definition of statehood as a monopoly on the legitimate use of violence.

16. The two cases are *The Prosecutor* v. *Uhuru Muigai Kenyatta,* ICC-01/09-02/11 (closed March 15, 2015), and *The Prosecutor* v. *William Samoei Ruto and Joshua Arap Sang,* ICC-01/09-01/11 (closed April 5, 2016). See www.icc-cpi.int/Pages/Situations .aspx (listing all ICC investigations and how they were initiated).

17. Commission of Inquiry on Post-Election Violence (CIPEV) ("Waki Commission"). Report available at http://kenyalaw.org/Downloads/Reports/Commission_ of_Inquiry_into_Post_Election_Violence.pdf.

18. United Nations Security Council Resolution S/RES/955 (1994), November 8, 1994, at www.unmict.org/specials/ictr-remembers/docs/res955-1994_en.pdf.

19. The political minefield accompanying consideration of Kagame's involvement in state-sponsored violence in and around Rwanda is discussed in depth in chapter 2. See also French (2009); Prunier (2010); Epstein (2017a).

20. Logan (2017).

21. Judgment in Application 003/2014, *Victoire Ingabire Umuhoza* v. *Republic of Rwanda*, African Court on Human and Peoples' Rights (AfCHPR) (November 24, 2017).

22. Burke (2019).

Chapter 1

1. For explanations focusing on state politics, see Clark (2018); Branch (2017); Brett and Gissel (2020); for an explanation regarding internal palace wars, see Bosco (2013); for wider considerations regarding African relations with former colonizers in the field of law, see Clarke (2009, 2019).

2. Overy (2003).

3. This phrase comes from Justice Robert H. Jackson's opening speech at the Nuremberg Trials, where he was a prosecutor.

4. Fukuyama (1992).

5. Regarding the Tokyo trials, as at Nuremberg, the Allied powers hosted a trial of their adversaries at Tokyo following the war. With eleven nations participating as judges, the Tokyo Tribunal was more diverse than the four-nation Nuremberg Tribunal, that is, it was more truly international. It was also very obviously political; for example, the emperor was excluded from the tribunal's mandate, because the Allies found him essential for managing the postwar peace. It also resulted in a non-unanimous verdict: Justice Radhabinod Pal of India wrote a 900-page dissent gaining him reverence in Japan. These are among the reasons that have contributed to its near absence in international criminal justice legacy circles. See Minear (1971); see also Röling and Cassese (1993).

6. Shapiro (1981).

7. All ICTY cases are available at www.icty.org/en/cases.

8. Statement of the ICC Prosecutor, March 3, 2021, available at www.icc-cpi.int/Pages/item.aspx?name=210303-prosecutor-statement-investigation-palestine.

9. ICC Pre-trial Chamber II, "Decision Pursuant to Article 15 of the Rome Statute on the Authorisation of an Investigation into the Situation in the Islamic Republic of Afghanistan," April 12, 2019, available at www.icc-cpi.int/CourtRecords/CR2019_02068.PDF

10. See preliminary investigation of the blockade of the Gaza strip, the "Registered Vessels of Comoros, Greece and Cambodia" investigation (www.icc-cpi.int/comoros), closed in 2014, appealed and redirected to the OTP on September 2, 2019.

11. This case dragged on until December 2019 when the prosecutor issued her "reconsideration" affirming the original decision on absence of gravity. This reconsideration was a result of the Appeals Chamber judgment of September 2, 2019, ordering the OTP to reconsider her office's decision not to move forward with the situation in light of judicial instructions issued in 2016. Even while ordering the OTP to reconsider, the Appeals Chambers decision re-affirmed by majority, three votes to two, that the prosecutor makes the "ultimate decision" regarding whether or not she initiates an investigation.

12. Rome Statute Article 17(1)(a).

13. See discussion on "positive complementarity" in Hobbs (2020).

14. See Council of Europe, "Supervision of the Execution of Judgments" (2007), available at www.osce.org/files/f/documents/a/c/33737.pdf; see also Shany (2014).

15. Dothan (2014).

16. For a discussion on the domestic political impact of ICC complementarity, see Nouwen (2013).

17. Rome Statute Article 17(2)(a); Rome Statute Article 17(2)(b); Rome Statute Article 17(2)(c).

18. *Case Concerning the Arrest Warrant of April 2000 (Democratic Republic of the Congo v. Belgium)*, International Court of Justice, February 14, 2002. The ICJ is the world's oldest international court and permits those states who consent to its jurisdiction to resolve differences between them juridically. It sits in the Peace Palace in The Hague.

19. Ibid., para 60.

20. Mamdani (1996).

21. Clarke (2009).

22. "Decision under article 87(7) of the Rome Statute on the non-compliance by South Africa with the request by the Court for the arrest and surrender of Omar Al-Bashir," ICC-02/05-01/09-302 (July 6, 2017).

23. The African Union's position, according to officials in its Office of Legal Counsel, should be understood as seeking power and control over African states' own affairs and not ceding that control to external forces with insufficient local knowledge or concern (interview with author, February 2013). This is not a coherent strategy, because, effectively, the African Union, a supranational governance organization, is opposed to the ICC, a supranational judicial organization, based on an argument that states should never be challenged in their dominance over internal affairs.

24. Judgment in the Jordan Referral re Al-Bashir Appeal ICC-02/05-01/09-397-Corr, May 6, 2019 (Appeals Chamber).

25. Sadat (2019).

26. White (2018).

27. Akande (2019).

28. A list compiled by the Swiss Hirondelle Foundation in May 2019 explains why these numbers are not as transparent as would be ideal; for example, the ICC lists all indictments, but some are for contempt of court, and not atrocity crimes. See list at www.justiceinfo.net/en/tribunals/icc/41532-welcome-to-the-icc-facts-and-figures.html.

29. The prosecutor has the burden of proving the defendant's guilt with certainty for the adjudicators. At the end of the prosecution's case, it is possible for the defense to bring a "no case to answer" motion, essentially arguing that the prosecutor has not met her burden of establishing the defendant's guilt. The question is not a factual one of whether the judges find the defendant not guilty, but rather if, as a matter of law, any court could possibly find the defendant guilty based on the evidence presented. To lose on a "no case to answer" motion indicates a significant failure on the part of the prosecution.

30. A key rule-of-law concept distinguishes "situations" from more directed investigations. Were the ICC to open investigations of particular actors, this might violate the presumption of innocence. For this reason, the ICC investigates "situations" before eventually producing indictments against individuals, which are prosecuted.

31. See Prunier (2010).

32. See www.unhcr.org/news/briefing/2021/8/611618344/unhcr-gravely-con cerned-systematic-sexual-violence-dr-congos-tanganyika.html.

33. International Crisis Group, "Africa's Seven Nation War," May 19, 1999, avail-able here: International Crisis Group, May 19, 1999; see also Prunier (2010); Epstein (2017a).

34. Lubanga's case was originally tied to that of Bosco Ntaganda; the cases were severed because the ICC had Lubanga in its custody, while Ntaganda remained at large. Ntaganda turned himself in to the U.S. Embassy in Kigale, Rwanda, in 2013 after an internal coup within his paramilitary group put his life at risk. In 2019 he was convicted by the ICC and received a thirty-year sentence, which is currently on appeal.

35. For an excellent discussion of the ICC's capture by the Kabila regime and its relationship to complementarity, see Labuda (2017).

36. Nancy Combs has written an extraordinary book detailing this process, *Fact-finding without Facts* (2010).

37. Kersten (2019).

38. Judgment on the Appeal of Mr Jean-Pierre Bemba Gombo against Trial Chamber III's "Judgment pursuant to Article 74 of the Statute," June 8, 2018, avail-able at www.icc-cpi.int/CourtRecords/CR2018_02984.PDF.

39. Ibid., para 110.

40. Ibid., para 3.

41. Ibid., para 46. This line of argument is not, so far, convincing many observers; Leila Sadat, for example, notes that it is inappropriate for the Appeals Chamber to substitute its judgment for a court that labored over 4.5 years, collected the testimony of seventy-seven witnesses, and produced a nearly 400-page decision. See Sadat (2018).

42. Judgment on the Appeal of Mr Jean-Pierre Bemba Gombo, para 170.

43. "Rupture" is the process by which the defense challenges the tribunal in every possible way. It is perhaps most notoriously epitomized by the obstreperous bane of the ICTY, the Serbian far-right politician Vojislav Šešelj, who defended himself and ultimately hectored the ICTY into releasing him. See Carlson (2018).

44. Judgment on the Appeal of Mr Jean-Pierre Bemba Gombo, para 5.

45. The full report is available here: www.knchr.org/Portals/0/Reports/Waki_Report.pdf.

46. "Indirect co-perpetration" is a means of "doing" crime (referred to as "com-mission" or "complicity" in legalese) and refers to criminal conspiracies leading to atrocity crimes in which defendants may have participated, but without personally engaging, in the violent acts.

47. Stewart (2013).

48. Ba (2014).

49. *The Prosecutor* v. *William Samoei Ruto and Joshua Arap Sang*, Case No. ICC-01/09-01/11 (Int'l Crim. Ct. April 5, 2016).

50. Kersten (2015).

51. See Peskin (2009).

52. The ICC has also issued an arrest warrant for Gbagbo's wife, but Côte d'Ivoire has not surrendered her. So far, the ICC has indicted neither Ouattara nor his supporters.

53. Many observers note the chilling similarities to Rwanda-type tactics in which ethnic groups are used to incite violence. Kenya has a history of ethnic violence related to elections that makes the violence the ICC addressed particularly significant.

54. For a more detailed study of the politics of impunity in Kenyan governance, see Gissel (2018), ch. 5.

Chapter 2

1. Rwanda has also withdrawn its signature on the protocol allowing individuals to bring cases against it before the African Court on Human and Peoples' Rights; see chapter 5 for discussion of this protocol and its import.

2. See BBC, "Rwanda's Paul Kigame, Visionary or Tyrant?," August 3, 2017 (www.bbc.com/news/10479882), which describes Kagame as a doer and effective politician and authoritarian. See also the World Bank's website on Rwanda, which summarizes the country with the heading, "Rwanda has achieved impressive development gains since the 1994 genocide and civil war," at www.worldbank.org/en/country/rwanda/overview.

3. See her autobiography written from her jail cell (Ingabire, 2017). Ingabire brought a claim before the African Court on Human and Peoples' Rights, which found in her favor in 2017. Rwanda has since withdrawn from the protocol allowing individuals to lodge a complaint with the court.

4. This includes several former Kagame allies. The latest victims include Ingabire's personal assistant, killed in March 2019. See Fröhlich (2019); Amnesty International (2019b).

5. Prunier (2010); Emizet (2000), pp. 163–202; Reyntjens (2009).

6. Lichter (2004); Prunier (2010); Rever (2018); Thomson (2018).

7. Convention on the Prevention and Punishment of the Crime of Genocide, United Nations, 1948, at https://treaties.un.org/doc/publication/unts/volume%2078/volume-78-i-1021-english.pdf.

8. In 2018 a UN-funded court, originally set up to try crimes committed by the Khmer Rouge in Cambodia, found a defendant guilty of genocide against Muslim and Vietnamese minority populations. See Lingaas (2020).

9. UN OHCHR, "Report of the Mapping Exercise documenting the most serious violations of human rights and international humanitarian law committed within the territory of the Democratic Republic of the Congo between March 1993 and June 2003" (2010), at www.ohchr.org/Documents/Countries/CD/DRC_MAPPING_REPORT_FINAL_EN.pdf. See also www.bbc.com/news/world-africa-11105289.

10. Akhavan (2012).

11. Schabas (2003).

12. See, for example, May (2010).

13. Epstein (2017b).

14. Eltingham (2004).

15. Wrong (2021).

16. Dallaire (2003).

17. See discussion in Epstein (2017a), pp. 101–14.

18. This is described in Gourevitch (1998).

19. See Dallaire (2003).

20. Human Rights Watch (1995); Prunier (2010).

21. Human Rights Watch (1999).

22. Uwera (2017).

23. Prunier (2010).

24. Melvern and others (2014).

25. Ibid.

26. Reyntjens (2014).

27. Reydams (2016).

28. See especially Van Oijin (2018) for a critical assessment of Reydams's position.

29. Melvern and others (2018).

30. De Waal (2016).

31. Savelsberg (2015), p. 2.

32. See discussion in Carlson (2018), ch. 5.

33. UN Security Council, Resolution 955 (1994), at https://undocs.org/S/RES/955(1994).

34. Off (2001); Eltingham (2019).

35. UN Security Council, Resolution 955 (1994).

36. Rwanda, U.N. Doc. S/RES/977 (1995), at http://hrlibrary.umn.edu/resolutions/SC95/977SC95.html.

37. Rwanda, U.N. Doc. S/RES/1165 (1998).

38. *The Prosecutor* v. *Jean-Paul Akayesu (Trial Judgement)*, ICTR-96-4-T, International Criminal Tribunal for Rwanda (ICTR), September 2, 1998; *The Prosecutor* v. *Jean-Paul Akayesu (Appeal Judgment)*, ICTR-96-4-A, International Criminal Tribunal for Rwanda (ICTR), June 1, 2001.

39. Van Schaak (2008).

40. *Akayesu Trial Judgement* 1998, paras. 187–193.

41. *Akayesu Trial Judgement* 1998, para. 12.

42. See UN's Genocide Convention 1948, Article II. See also Rovetta (2014); de Brouwer (2005); and Mitchell and Louvel (2015).

43. Kambanda pleaded guilty to incitement to genocide. He had been hastily sworn in as prime minister in April 1994 on the death of the Rwanda president in the plane crash. Leader of the Hutu extremist movement that advocated Hutu dominance in politics, Kambanda received a life sentence and is serving this in Mali.

Kambanda's plea was entered one week after Rwandan officials (some of whom were Kambanda associates) publicly executed twenty-two people found guilty of participating in the genocide. Under ICTR rules of procedure, Kambanda's guilty plea precluded him from being tried in Rwanda.

44. The trial chamber sentenced Nahimana and Ngeze to life, although the sentences were reduced to thirty and thirty-five years, respectively, and Barayagwiza got thirty-five years.

45. Milmo (2008).

46. Bagosora was tried with three others, one of whom was acquitted in the ICTR's 2008 trial chamber judgment. *The Prosecutor* v. *Bagosora*, ICTR-98-41-T, International Criminal Tribunal for Rwanda (ICTR), December 18, 2008 (https://unictr.irmct.org/en/cases/ictr-98-41). The process was quite long, prompting criticism from observers; see Schabas (2008).

47. "Letter Dated 1 October 1994 from the Secretary-General Addressed to the President of the Security Council," UNSC, *S/1994/1125* (1994). See also Human Rights Watch (1996).

48. Peskin (2005).

49. Off (2001). See also Peskin (2005); Rever (2018); Vidal (2018).

50. del Ponte, with Sudetic (2009).

51. Ibid.

52. Peskin (2008); Des Forges (1999); Mamdani (2002).

53. Ryngaert (2013).

54. Human Rights Watch (2011).

55. Clark (2010); Ingelaere (2012; 2016).

56. Human Rights Watch (2011).

57. Palmer (2015).

58. Ibid., p. 46.

59. See Palmer (2015); Straus (2006); Hintjens (2008); Thomson (2018); Mamdani (1996), (2002).

60. Hintjens (2008), p 5.

61. Thomson (2018), p. 13.

62. Rever (2018). Regarding popular press reaction to Rever, see also Epstein (2018).

63. Vidal (2018).

64. Thomson (2018).

65. Kelsall (2013).

66. France was given jurisdiction because of the three French crew members who died on the flight.

67. See discussion in Maison and de La Pradelle (2014).

68. See *Case Concerning the Arrest Warrant of 11 April 2000 (Democratic Republic of the Congo* v. *Belgium)*, International Court of Justice (ICJ), February 11, 2002.

69. In 2019 French president Emmanuel Macron appointed eight historians to an investigatory committee tasked with investigating France's role in the lead-up to the

genocide. The report found France erred but was not complicit in the genocide. See Duclert (2021). Macron has promised to open the French archives regarding the genocide. In 2015 President Holland had also promised to open the archives, but a request for review by a researcher was denied by France's highest court in 2017. See Décision n° 2017-655 QPC du 15 septembre 2017 (www.conseil-constitutionnel.fr/decision/2017/2017655QPC.htm).

70. The 2006 French investigation of the downed presidential plane implicated Nyamwasa himself, who also had been indicted by a Spanish court in conjunction with genocidal violence while working for the RPF. In 2011 he was tried in absentia in a Rwandan court and sentenced to twenty-four years in jail for "disturbing public order, damage to state security, libel and defamation, bigotry and conspiracy." See summary of cases at Trial International at https://trialinternational.org/latest-post/faustin-kayumba-nyamwasa/.

71. For a long exposé on the case, see Wrong (2019).

72. See Peskin (2008). See also a review of several aspects of Rwanda in Stys (2012), as well as Hintjens (2008).

73. Rever (2018); Thomson (2018); Sundaram (2016).

74. Jaji (2017).

Chapter 3

1. Weill, Seelinger, and Carlson (2020).

2. This dichotomy is drawn from the work of Scott (1999), discussed further in chapter 4.

3. This is known as the "Claustre affair."

4. Human Rights Watch has written a great deal, in English, regarding Habré's regime and its methods. See, for example, Bercault (2013). Former prisoners have written narratives of their experience, in French. See, for example, Souleymane Guengueng's account in Guengueng (2013).

5. For a discussion, see Toïngar (2006).

6. Rapport de la Commission d'enquête nationale du Ministère tchadien de la Justice (Report by the Commission of National Investigation of the Chadian Ministry of Justice), *Les crimes et detournments de l'ex President Habré et de ses complices*, 1993 (published by Editions L'Harmattan, Paris), hereafter the Truth Commission Report.

7. Abakar (2020); Truth Commission Report (1993).

8. The Truth Commission Report labeled deaths under Habré "genocide" (p. 39). See also Abakar (2020). There is an English language summary of the commission's work at www.usip.org/sites/default/files/file/resources/collections/commissions/Chad-Report.pdf.

9. Truth Commission Report (1993). The commission's ultimate estimate of 40,000 dead is based on the 3,780 people it concretely determined were killed (p. 69); its estimate that such a number represented one-tenth of the actual damage done by Habré (p. 69); and a rounding up from 37,000 to 40,000 (p. 97).

10. Human Rights Watch and two judicial fact-finding missions found numbers far below the 40,000 figure. HRW, for example, found that 1,208 people were killed or died in detention. See www.hrw.org/news/2014/11/10/chad-alleged-habre-accom plices-stand-trial.

11. Abakar (2020).

12. See, for example, recent research by Bat, Duranton, El Ghaziri, Sigalas, and Stemmelin (2019) that shows how Habré's surveillance state continued under Déby.

13. Thulliez (2020).

14. Ibid.

15. Robinson (2004), p. 16.

16. *Ministere Public* v. *Hissene Habré*, Cour d'Appel Dakar, Chambre d'Accussation, Arret No 135 (April 7, 2000).

17. *Souleyman Guengueng* v. *Hissène Habré*, Cour de Cassation, Criminal Arret No. 14 (March 20, 2001) (Sen). See also the chapter discussing the case written by Hélène Cissé, attorney for Habré from 2000 to 2004: Cissé (2020).

18. Committee Against Torture, Decisions of the Committee Against Torture under Article 22 of the Convention against Torture and Other Cruel, Inhuman or Degrading Treatment or Punishment, Paras 9.6-9.12, U.N. Doc. CAT/C/36/D181 /2001 (May 19, 2006).

19. Loi No. 2008–23 du 25 juillet 2008 de portant insertion d'un article 664 bis dans le Code de Procédure pénale [Law 2008–23 of July 25, 2008, on the insertion of Article 664 bis of the Code of Criminal Procedure], *Journal Officiel de la République du Senegal*, July 25, 2008 (Sen.), at www.jo.gouv.sn/spip.php?article7102; Loi Constitutionnelle No. 2008–30 du 7 août 2008 de modifiant les articles 7, 63, 68, 71, et 82 de la Constitution [Law 2008–30 of August 7, 2008, amending Articles 7, 63, 68, 71, and 82 of the Constitution], *Journal Officiel de la République du Senegal*, August 7, 2008 (Sen.), at www.gouv.sn/Loi-Constitutionnelle-modifiant,707.html.

20. *Hissein Habré* v. *Republic of Senegal*, Case No. ECW/CCJ/APP/07/08, Judgment ECOWAS Community Court of Justice, November 10, 2010.

21. Application No. 001/2008—*Michelot Yogogombaye* v. *The Republic of Senegal*; for helpful background, see Barrie Sander, Case Summary, December 7, 2011, at http://arcproject.co.uk/wp-content/uploads/2013/04/CSW-001-2008.pdf.

22. Senegal is a signatory of the UN's Convention Against Torture. In 2006 a UN committee ruling in the case, *Guengueng* v. *Senegal*, found that Senegal was in breach of its obligations under the Convention Against Torture and must either prosecute or extradite Habré. Available at www.unhchr.ch/tbs/doc.nsf/(Symbol)/aafdd8e81a424 894c125718c004490f6?Opendocument.

23. *Questions relating to the Obligation to Prosecute or Extradite (Belgium* v. *Senegal)* Judgment (July 20, 2012), 51 ILM 706.

24. Agreement of the Establishment of the Extraordinary African Chambers within the Sengalese Judicial System between the Government of the Republic of Senegal and the African Union, August 22, 2012, 52 I.L.M. 1024 (2013).

25. Dickinson (2003); Williams (2016).

26. Christensen (2015).

27. Brett and Gissel (2020).

28. Fichtelberg (2015).

29. For the Lebanon case, see www.stl-tsl.org/en/; for Cambodia, see www.eccc. gov.kh/en; for Sierra Leone, see www.rscsl.org/; see also summaries regarding hybridity at www.internationalcrimesdatabase.org/Courts/Hybrid, and discussion in Dickenson (2003), as well as Fichtelberg (2015).

30. Daily summaries of witness testimony are available in English on the website of Trust Africa, a local NGO that monitored the trial: www.ijmonitor.org/2016/02/hissene-habre-trial-before-the-extraordinary-african-chambers-december-hearings/.

31. Human Rights Watch, www.hrw.org/news/2015/10/22/senegal-hissene-habre-trial-sexual-slavery-accounts.

32. Ohlin (2009); Goy (2012).

33. The broad application of JCE changed, however, as more senior leaders came under review, beginning about fifteen years into the ICTY's practice. Then the doctrine narrowed and became more limited as JCE was applied to senior leaders. For an examination of this evolution, see chapter 4 in Carlson (2018).

34. Carlson (2018).

35. Editorial Board, "A Milestone for Justice in Africa," *New York Times*, July 22, 2015.

36. Sikkink (2011); Allott (1990).

37. See the Indictment, "Ordonnance de Non-Lieu Partiel, de mise en Accusation et de Renvoi devant la Chambre Africaine Extraordinaire d'Assises," at www.chambresafricaines.org/pdf/OrdonnanceRenvoi_CAE_13022015.pdf.

38. This is the argument put forward by Brad Roth in his contestation of universal jurisdiction. See Roth (2010).

39. In Senegal it is not uncommon for men with means to support several wives and, therefore, several households.

Chapter 4

1. An estimated 1.7 million are internally displaced and 2.2 million externally displaced. See UNHCR statistics on South Sudan at https://data2.unhcr.org/en/situations/southsudan#_ga=2.47700644.2074930584.1551256287-1470138429.1551256287.

2. Revitalized Agreement on the Resolution of the Conflict in the Republic of South Sudan at https://igad.int/programs/115-south-sudan-office/1950-signed-revitalized-agreement-on-the-resolution-of-the-conflict-in-south-sudan.

3. The success of the R-ARCSS should not be understood to be synonymous with peace. The UN Commission for South Sudan's March 2020 report, for example, begins by detailing government corruption leading to starvation on a massive scale: "more than half of South Sudan's population has been deliberately starved of food while their leaders brazenly looted and plundered the country's wealth." The report goes on to state: "The Commission is concerned that the international community

may be lulled into believing that the conflict is fully over, now that a unity government has been formed in South Sudan. The reality on the ground is much more complex and while the revitalized peace process has led to a fragile peace at the national level in South Sudan, the conflict has morphed into localized conflicts in which ethnic divisions are being mobilised, resulting in a 200% increase in the number of civilian casualties in 2019 over the previous year." Read the full report here: https://reliefweb.int/report/south-sudan/statement-yasmin-sooka-chair-un -commission-human-rights-south-sudan-human-rights.

4. Article 16 of the ICC allows for one-year deferral and does not limit how many successive deferrals may be applied. Thus, Article 16 effectively grants unlimited deferral powers to the UN Security Council. As of this writing, the UNSC has never engaged Article 16, although some countries have requested that it do so.

5. See Mbeki and Mamdani (2014); Kiir and Machar (2016). Author interviews with employees of nongovernmental organizations and International Governmental Organization (IGO) employees, April 2019, Addis Ababa; notes on file.

6. Transitional justice is a significant field with a vast literature. Some of the central works include Israël and Mouralis (2014); Teitel (2000); Hazan (2000; 2008); Kritz (1995); Olsen, Payne, and Reiter (2010); Huyse (1995); Elster (2004); Quinn (2009); Sharp (2018).

7. Gissel (2017).

8. See statement of Prosecutor, September 1, 2016, at www.icc-cpi.int/Pages/item .aspx?name=160901-otp-stat-colombia; see also Close (2016); Aksenova (2018).

9. Bell (2016); Carlson (2018); Daly (2017); Gissel (2017); Sharp (2018); Subotic (2013).

10. Kelsall (2013).

11. Daly (2017).

12. Recall political scientist Francis Fukuyama's 1992 claim that democracy had beaten totalitarianism, and we were witnessing an end of history. This claim has proven premature.

13. The most ardent is Hannah Arendt, who in 1951, in *The Origins of Totalitarianism*, explained that only the state can create conditions within which people can be meaningfully (that is, politically) recognized as human.

14. Fichtelberg (2015).

15. Final Report on the African Union Commission of Inquiry for South Sudan. Addis Ababa, October 15, 2014, at www.peaceau.org/uploads/auciss.final.report.pdf.

16. Ibid., para 834.

17. Author interviews, April 2019, Addis Ababa; notes on file.

18. See also Prunier (2010) regarding state networks of violence in central Africa.

19. "Security Council Press Statement on Sexual Violence in South Sudan," December 7, 2018, at https://unmiss.unmissions.org/sites/default/files/security_council _press_statement_on_sexual_violence_in_south_sudan.pdf.

20. "Civilians deliberately and brutally targeted during surge in conflict in Cen-

tral Equatoria," July 3, 2019, at https://unmiss.unmissions.org/sites/default/files/press_release_central_equatoria_-_final.pdf.

21. Beaumont (2018). In her report for the Council of Foreign Relations, Knopf (2016) detailed the balkanization of military forces in South Sudan as a central challenge to achieving and maintaining peace.

22. Boswell (2019).

23. Mednick (2019).

24. Rolandsen (2011).

25. Moro (2006).

26. Rolandsen (2015).

27. *The Economist*, "Crisis in South Sudan: The Promise and Peril of Independence," June 11, 2011, at www.economist.com/middle-east-and-africa/2009/06/11/the-promise-and-peril-of-independence.

28. Author interview, April 2019, Addis Ababa; notes on file.

29. The reports can all be accessed here: https://unmiss.unmissions.org/human-rights-reports.

30. Doki (2014).

31. Foltyn (2016). This incident joined other complaints, including reports that women had been raped outside the camp's entrance, in plain view of the camp.

32. Associated Press, "UN Peacekeepers in South Sudan 'Ignored Rape and Assault of Aid Workers,'" *The Guardian*, August 15, 2016, at www.theguardian.com/world/2016/aug/15/south-sudan-aid-worker-rape-attack-united-nations-un.

33. Amnesty International (2019a).

34. Knopf (2016); Boswell (2019); author interview with South Sudanese diplomat, April 2019, Addis Ababa; notes on file. The official stressed the necessity of one unified army as the key to peace under the R-ARCSS.

35. For example, investigating judges working on the hybrid court in Senegal that tried Hissène Habré in 2015 (see chapter 3) considered tracing his ill-gotten gains in order to add monies to a fund for victims, but determined that they did not have jurisdiction.

36. R-ARCSS 5.3.1.1 (emphasis added).

37. ARCSS 3.3.2; R-ARCSS 5.3.3.2.

38. ARCSS 3.3.3; R-ARCSS 5.3.3.3.

39. ARCSS 3.3.6; R-ARCSS 5.3.3.6.

40. Commencing its seventh mission to South Sudan in August 2019, UNHRC representative Barney Afako reiterated: "The lack of progress in establishing transitional justice mechanisms, including the Hybrid Court, the commission for truth, reconciliation, and healing and the compensation and reparation authority, which are to be complemented by customary and other community-centred mechanisms, is delaying accountability and reparation for these and other crimes. So long as the voices of victims and survivors are not empowered, and these mechanisms not put in place, it is highly unlikely that South Sudanese women, men, girls, and boys will be able to witness

a lasting peace." United Nations Human Rights Council, August 23, 2019, www.ohchr
.org/EN/HRBodies/HRC/Pages/NewsDetail.aspx?NewsID=24914&LangID=E.

41. Chairperson Yasmin Sooka noted, "A key element in our report is that sustainable peace requires a tangible and credible pursuit of accountability and justice that
meets the needs of the many thousands of victims. The lack of accountability for
decades of violence during the struggle for independence helped to fuel the current
conflict in South Sudan." United Nations Human Rights Council, February 20,
2019, www.ohchr.org/EN/HRBodies/HRC/Pages/NewsDetail.aspx?NewsID=
24184&LangID=E.

42. Mbeki and Mamdani (2014).

43. Human Rights Council (2019).

44. Okuk (2018).

45. Massoud (2013); Kindersley (2019), p. 67.

Chapter 5

1. Author interview with representatives from PALU, May 2019, Arusha.

2. Author interview with representatives from the African Institute for International Law, May 2019, Arusha.

3. Dothan (2014).

4. This is a challenge faced by many international organizations, which are created by states and have their own agency and identity. See Klabbers (2015).

5. Protocol of Tribunal in the Southern African Development Community,
August 7, 2000, at www.sadc.int/files/1413/5292/8369/Protocol_on_the_Tribunal_
and_Rules_thereof2000.pdf.

6. Declaration and Treaty of SADC (1992), www.wipo.int/edocs/lexdocs/treaties
/en/sadc/trt_sadc.pdf.

7. Meredith (2003).

8. *Mike Campbell (Pvt) Ltd and Others* v. *Republic of Zimbabwe* (2/2007) [2008]
SADCT 2 (28 November 2008).

9. Hulse (2012).

10. *Law Society of South Africa and Others* v. *President of the Republic of South
Africa and Others* [2018] ZACC 51.

11. See, for example, Fabricus (2019).

12. Author interview, May 2019, Arusha.

13. Taye (2018). See also Mamdani (1996), examining how colonial structures
impact contemporary social and political organization in African countries. Throughout the twentieth century, east Africa was closely watched in relation to its potential
for regional integration. See, for example, Segal (1965).

14. Gathii (2013).

15. Possi (2016).

16. *Prof. Peter Anyang' Nyong'o and 10 Others* v. *Attorney General of the Republic of
Kenya and 5 Others* (Reference No. 1 of 2006 [Ruling]) [2006] EACJ 3 November
27, 2006, at www1.saflii.org/ea/cases/EACJ/2006/3.pdf.

17. See extensive discussion in Alter, Gathi, and Helfer (2016).

18. Apiko (2017).

19. *Prof. Peter Anyang' Nyong'o and Others* v. *Attorney General of Kenya and Others* (Reference No. 1 of 2006 (Judgment)) [2007] EACJ 6 (30 March 2007), para. 114, at http://www.worldcourts.com/eacj/eng/decisions/2007.03.30_Nyong_o_v_ Attorney_General_Kenya.htm.

20. See the EACJ's first case, *Mwatela and Others* v. *East African Community* (Application No. 1 of 2005) [2006] EACJ 1 (1 October 2006), and its demonstration of judicial activism.

21. *East African Law Society* v. *The Republic of Uganda and Another* (Reference No. 2 of 2011) [2018], March 28, 2018.

22. Author interview at EACJ, May 2019, Arusha.

23. Ibid.

24. Taye (2020).

25. *Prof. Nyamoya Francois* v. *The Attorney General of the Republic of Burundi*, Reference No. 8 of 2011 (EACJ, February 28, 2014); *Omar Awadh and Six Others* v. *Attorney General of Kenya, Attorney General of Uganda, and Secretary General of the EAC*, App. No. 4 of 2011 (EACJ, November 1, 2011).

26. *Steven Dennis* v. *The Attorney General of the Republic of Burundi and Others*, Reference No. 3/2015 March 31, 2017; Possi (2017).

27. Ebobrah (2007).

28. *James Katabazi and 21 Others* v. *Secretary General of the East African Community and Attorney General of the Republic of Uganda* (Reference No. 1 of 2007) [2007] EACJ 3 (1 November 2007).

29. Ebobrah (2009).

30. Article 8 concerns the general obligations of the partner states to take necessary steps to realize the treaty and to avoid setting up obstacles to the fulfilment of its objectives. Articles 29 and 71 address the role played by the Secretariat. The relevant element of Article 29 is its beginning, which reads "Where the Secretary General considers that a Partner State has failed . . ." The relevant part of Article 71 was part (1)(d), which reads: "1. The Secretariat shall be responsible for: the undertaking either on its own initiative or otherwise, of such investigations, collection of information, or verification of matters *relating to any matter affecting the Community* that appears to it to merit examination."

31. *James Katabazi and 21 Others* v. *Secretary General of the East African Community and Attorney General of the Republic of Uganda.*

32. *Democratic Party* v. *The Secretary General of the EAC*, Appeal No. 1 of 2014 (*Democratic Party* case). Ally Possi (2016) argues that with this case, the EACJ's human rights jurisdiction mandate has become "official."

33. A full list of EACJ human rights decisions, and descriptions of them, as of May 2018, is available in Taye (2018).

34. Open Society Justice Initiative (2015).

35. See *MSETO and Hali Halisi Publishers Ltd* v. *The Attorney General of the Re-*

public of Tanzania, Reference No. 7 of 2016 (EACJ, June 21, 2018). This is a freedom of expression case concerning a Tanzania newspaper. It is only a first instance court decision (trial court); the appeals court decision is pending.

36. *Democratic Party* v. *The Secretary General of the EAC and Four Others*, Reference No. 2 of 2012 (29 November 2013).

37. Author interview, judge on the EACJ, May 2019, Arusha.

38. Author interview, local human rights organizations, May 2019, Arusha.

39. Quote attributed to Jakaya Kikwete, Tanzanian president (2005–2015), regarding the SADC tribunal, in Christie (2011).

40. de Tocqueville (2002).

Conclusion

1. See the map at "Alkebu-lan: If Africa Was Never Colonized by Europe," *The Decolonial Atlas* (blog), November 15, 2014, https://decolonialatlas.wordpress.com/2014/11/15/alkebu-lan-1260-ah/.

2. See "The Upsidedown Map Page," www.flourish.org/upsidedownmap/.

3. Protocol on Amendments to the Protocol on the Statute of the African Court of Justice and Human Rights ("Malabo Protocol"), June 27, 2014, https://au.int/en/treaties/protocol-amendments-protocol-statute-african-court-justice-and-human-rights.

4. See, for example, de Silva and Holthoefer (2019).

5. Author interview with Don Deya, May 2019, Arusha; notes on file.

6. Dersso (2016).

7. Sirleaf (2017); Prosperi and Terrosi (2017).

8. See the complete transcription from December 10, 2019, at www.icj-cij.org/files/case-related/178/178-20191210-ORA-01-00-BI.pdf.

9. See the complete transcription from December 11, 2019, at www.icj-cij.org/files/case-related/178/178-20191211-ORA-01-00-BI.pdf.

References

Abakar, Mahamat Hassan. 2020. "The Making of Chad's Truth Commission." In *The President On Trial: Prosecuting Hissène Habré*, edited by Sharon Weil, Kim Thuy Seelinger, and Kerstin Bree Carlson. Oxford University Press.

Abel, Richard L. 2018. *Law's Trials: The Performance of Legal Institutions in the US "War on Terror."* Cambridge University Press.

Akande, Dapo. 2019. "ICC Appeals Chamber Holds that Heads of State Have No Immunity under Customary International Law Before International Tribunals." May 6, www.ejiltalk.org/.

Akhavan, Payam. 2012. *Reducing Genocide to Law: Definition, Meaning, and the Ultimate Crime.* Cambridge University Press.

Aksenova, Marina. 2018. "The ICC Involvement in Colombia: Walking the Fine Line between Peace and Justice." In *Quality Control in Preliminary Examination: Volume 1*, edited by Morten Bergsmo and Carsten Stahn. Torkel Opsahl Academic Epublisher.

Allott, Phillip. 1990. *Eunomia.* Oxford University Press.

Amnesty International. 2019a. "South Sudan: Missing File Blocks Justice for Terrain Hotel Rapes and Murder." September 6, www.amnesty.org/en/latest/news/2019 /09/south-sudan-missing-file-blocks-justice-for-terrain-hotel-rapes-murder/.

———. 2019b. "Rwanda: Opposition Politician Stabbed to Death in Latest 'Suspicious' Attack." September 24, www.amnesty.org.uk/press-releases/rwanda-oppo sition-politician-stabbed-death-latest-suspicious-attack.

Apiko, Philomena. 2017. "Understanding the East African Court of Justice: The Hard Road to Independent Institutions and Human Rights Jurisdiction." European Centre for Development Policy Management.

March, https://ecdpm.org/wp-content/uploads/EACJ-Background-Paper-PEDRO -Political-Economy-Dynamics-Regional-Organisations-Africa-ECDPM-2017. pdf.

Arendt, Hannah. 1951. *The Origins of Totalitarianism.* Schocken Books.

Ba, Oumar. 2014. "Kenyatta Went to The Hague: How to Bet and Win against the (International) System." October 20, https://africasacountry.com/2014/10/ken yatta-went-to-the-hague-how-to-bet-and-win-against-the-international-system.

Bat, Jean-Pierre, Antoine Duranton, Soheila El Ghaziri, Mathilde Sigalas, and Margo Stemmelin. 2019. "Renseigner et administrer la terreur sous Hissein Habré: la Direction de la documentation et de la sécurité." 17 *Champ Pénal* (Penal Field), https://journals.openedition.org/champpenal/10789 (in French).

Beaumont, Peter. 2018. "Born out of Brutality, South Sudan, the World's Youngest States, Drowns in Murder, Rape and Arson." *The Guardian*, June 24, www.the guardian.com/global-development/2018/jun/24/south-sudan-civil-war-refugees -families-flee-murder-rape-arson-nyal-global-development.

Bell, Christine. 2016. "The Fabric of Transitional Justice: Binding Local and Global Political Settlements." From *Transitional Justice* (Routledge), published at https:/ /papers.ssrn.com/abstract=2850418.

Bercault, Olivier. 2013. *Plain of the Dead: The Chad of Hissène Habré (1982–1990)*. Human Rights Watch.

Bosco, David. 2013. *Rough Justice: The International Criminal Court in a World of Power Politics*. Oxford University Press.

Boswell, Alan. 2019. "The Perils of Payroll Peace." London School of Economics. March, https://sites.tufts.edu/reinventingpeace/files/2019/03/The-Perils-of -Payroll-Peace.pdf.

Branch, Adam. 2017. "Dominic Ongwen on Trial: The ICC's African Dilemmas." *International Journal of Transitional Justice* 11, no. 1.

Brett, Peter, and Line Engbo Gissel. 2020. *Africa and the Backlash against International Courts*. Zed Books.

de Brouwer, Anne-Marie. 2005. *Supranational Criminal Prosecution of Sexual Violence: The ICC and the Practice of the ICTY and ICTR*. Interstitia.

Burgorgue-Larsen, Laurence. 2019. "Populism and Human Rights from Disenchantment to Democratic Riposte." *iCourts Working Paper Series*, no. 156. University of Copenhagen, available at https://papers.ssrn.com/sol3/papers.cfm?abstract_ id=3341298.

Burke, Jason. 2019. "Rwanda Opposition Leader Says Ally's Killing Was Act of Intimidation." *The Guardian*, September 25, www.theguardian.com/world/2019/ sep/25/rwanda-opposition-leader-victoire-ingabire-ally-killing-act-intimidation.

Carlson, Kerstin Bree. 2018. *Model(ing) Justice: Perfecting the Promise of International Criminal Law*. Cambridge University Press.

Caserta, Salvatore, and Pola Cebulak. 2018. "The Limits of International Adjudication: Authority and Resistance of Regional Economic Courts in Times of Crisis." *International Journal of Law in Context* 14, no. 2.

Christensen, Mikkel Jarle. 2015. "The Emerging Sociology of International Criminal Courts: Between Global Restructurings and Scientific Innovations." *Current Sociology* 63, no. 6: 825–49.

Christie, Sean. 2011. "Killed off by 'Kings and Potentates.'" *Mail and Guardian*.

August 19, https://mg.co.za/article/2011-08-19-killed-off-by-kings-and-poten
tates.

Cissé, Hélène. 2020. "Defending Habré in Senegal During the Early Years." In *The
President on Trial: Prosecuting Hissène Habré*, edited by Sharon Weill, Kim Thuy
Seelinger, and Kerstin Bree Carlson. Oxford University Press.

Clark, Phil. 2010. *The Gacaca Courts, Post-Genocide Justice and Reconciliation in
Rwanda: Justice without Lawyers*. Cambridge University Press.

———. 2018. *Distant Justice: The Impact of the International Criminal Court on African Politics*. Cambridge University Press.

Clarke, M. Kamari. 2009. *Fictions of Justice: The International Criminal Court and
the Challenge of Legal Pluralism in Sub-Sahara Africa*. Cambridge University
Press.

———. 2019. *Affective Justice: The International Criminal Court and the Pan-
Africanist Pushback*. Duke University Press.

Clausewitz, Carl Von. 1989. *On War*. Translated by Michael Eliot Howard and Peter
Paret. Princeton University Press.

Close, Josepha. 2016. "Meeting International Standards: Amnesty in the Colombian
Peace Deal." *Justice in Conflict* (blog). October 14, at https://justiceinconflict.org
/2016/10/14/meeting-international-standards-amnesty-in-the-colombian-peace
-deal/.

Combs, Nancy. 2010. *Factfinding without Facts: The Uncertain Evidentiary Foundations of International Criminal Convictions*. Cambridge University Press.

Cover, Robert. 1995. *Narrative, Violence, and the Law: The Essays of Robert Cover*,
edited by Martha Minow, Michael Ryan, and Austin Sarat. University of Michigan Press.

Dallaire, Romeo. 2003. *Shake Hands with the Devil: The Failure of Humanity in
Rwanda*. Random House.

Daly, Thomas Gerald. 2017. *The Alchemists: Questioning Our Faith in Courts as
Democracy-Builders*. Cambridge University Press.

Dersso, Solomon Ayele. 2016. "Unconstitutional Changes of Government and Unconstitutional Practices in Africa." *African Politics, African Peace*. June, https://
sites.tufts.edu/wpf/files/2017/07/2.-UCG-Dersso-f.pdf.

Des Forges, Alison Liebhafsky. 1999. *Leave None to Tell the Story: Genocide in
Rwanda*. Human Rights Watch.

de Waal, Alex. 2016. "Writing Human Rights and Getting It Wrong." *Boston Review*.
June 6, https://bostonreview.net/world/alex-de-waal-writing-human-rights.

Dickinson, Laura. 2003. "The Promise of Hybrid Courts." *American Journal of International Law* 97, no. 2: 295–310.

Doki, Charlton. 2014. "South Sudan Officials Blame UN for Deadly Attack in Bor."
Voice of Africa News. April 18, www.voanews.com/africa/south-sudan-officials
-blame-un-deadly-attack-bor.

Dothan, Shai. 2014. *Reputation and Judicial Tactics*. Cambridge University Press.

Duclert, Vincent. 2021. "La France, le Rwanda et le génocide des Tutsi (1990–1994):

Rapport remis au Président de la République." www.vie-publique.fr/rapport/279186-rapport-duclert-la-france-le-rwanda-et-le-genocide-des-tutsi-1990-1994.

Ebobrah, Solomon T. 2007. "A Rights-Protection Goldmine or a Waiting Volcanic Eruption? Competence of, and Access to, the Human Rights Jurisdiction of the ECOWAS Community Court of Justice." *African Human Rights Law Journal* 7, no. 2.

———. 2009. "Litigating Human Rights before Sub-Regional Courts in Africa." *African Journal International and Comparative Law* 17: 82–83.

Elster, Jon. 2004. *Closing the Books: Transitional Justice in Historical Perspective*. Cambridge University Press.

Eltingham, Nigel. 2004. *Accounting for Horror: Post Genocide Debates in Rwanda*. Pluto Press.

———. 2019. *Genocide Never Sleeps: Living Law at the International Criminal Tribunal for Rwanda*. Cambridge University Press.

Emizet, Kisangani N. F. 2000. "The Massacre of Refugees in Congo: A Case of UN Peacekeeping Failure and International Law." *Journal of Modern African Studies* 38, no. 2 (June): 163–202.

Epstein, Helen C. 2017a. *Another Fine Mess: America, Uganda, and the War on Terror*. Colombia Special Reports.

———. 2017b. "America's Secret Role in the Rwandan Genocide." *The Guardian*. September 12.

———. 2018. "A Deathly Hush." *New York Review of Books*. June 28.

Fabricus, Peter. 2019. "Will South Africa Fight for the SADC Tribunal's Revival?" Institute for Security Studies. September 6, https://issafrica.org/iss-today/will-south-africa-fight-for-the-sadc-tribunals-revival.

Fichtelberg, Aaron. 2015. *Hybrid Tribunals: A Comparative Examination*. Springer.

Foltyn, Simona. 2016. "'I Begged Them to Kill Me Instead': Women in South Sudan Raped under Nose of UN." *The Guardian*. July 29, www.theguardian.com/global-development/2016/jul/29/women-south-sudan-raped-un-compound-juba-kill-me-instead.

French, Howard W. 2009. "Kagame's Hidden War in the Congo." *New York Review of Books*. September 24, www.nybooks.com/articles/2009/09/24/kagames-hidden-war-in-the-congo/.

Fröhlich, Silja. 2019. "Rwanda's Disappearing Opposition." *DW*. August 5, www.dw.com/en/rwandas-disappearing-opposition/a-49887045.

Fukuyama, Francis. 1992. *The End of History and the Last Man*. Free Press.

Gathii, James. 2013. "Mission Creep or a Search for Relevance: The East African Court of Justice's Human Rights Strategy." *Duke Journal of Comparative and International Law* 24, no. 2.

Gissel, Line Engbo. 2017. "Contemporary Transitional Justice: Normalising a Politics of Exception." *Global Society* 31, no. 3: 353–69.

———. 2018. *The International Criminal Court and Peace Processes in Africa: Judicialising Peace*. Routledge.

Gourevitch, Philip. 1998. *We Wish to Inform You That Tomorrow We Will Be Killed with Our Families*. Farrar, Straus and Giroux.

Goy, Barbara. 2012. "Individual Criminal Responsibility before the International Criminal Court: A Comparison with the *Ad Hoc* Tribunals." *International Criminal Law Review* 12, no. 1.

Guengueng, Souleyman. 2013. *Prisonnier de Hissène Habré*. L'Harmattan.

Hazan, Pierre. 2000. *La Justice Face a la Guerre: De Nuremberg a La Haye*. Paris: Stock.

———. 2008. "Les Dilemmes de la Justice Transitionnelle." *Mouvements* 1, no. 53: 41–47.

Hintjens, Helen. 2008. "Post-Genocide Identity Politics in Rwanda." *Ethnicities* 8.1: 5–41.

Hobbs, Patricia. 2020. "The Catalysing Effect of the Rome Statute in Africa: Positive Complementarity and Self-Referrals." *Criminal Law Forum* 31: 345–376.

Human Rights Council. 2019. "Report of the Commission on Human Rights in South Sudan." March 19, A_HRC_40_69.

Human Rights Watch. 1995. *Human Rights Watch World Report 1995—Rwanda*. January 1, www.refworld.org/docid/467fca9dc.html.

———. 1996. "Shattered Lives: Sexual Violence during the Rwandan Genocide and Its Aftermath." www.hrw.org/reports/1996/Rwanda.htm.

———. 1999. "The Rwandan Patriotic Front." www.hrw.org/reports/1999/rwanda/Geno15-8-03.htm#P1015_314152.

———. 2011. "Justice Compromised: The Legacy of Rwanda's Community-Based Gacaca Courts." May 31, www.hrw.org/report/2011/05/31/justice-compromised/legacy-rwandas-community-based-gacaca-courts.

Hulse, Merran. 2012. "Silencing a Supranational Court: The Rise and Fall of the SADC Tribunal." *E-International Relations*. October 25, www.e-ir.info/2012/10/25/silencing-a-supranational-court-the-rise-and-fall-of-the-sadc-tribunal/.

Huyse, Luc. 1995. "Justice after Transition: On the Choices Successor Elites Make in Dealing with the Past." *Law and Social Inquiry* 20, no. 1: 51–78.

Ingabire, Victoire. 2017. *Between 4 Walls of the 1930 Prison: Memoirs of a Rwandan Prisoner of Conscience*. CreateSpace Independent Publishing Platform.

Ingelaere, Bert. 2012. "From Model to Practice: Researching and Representing Rwanda's 'Modernized' *Gacaca* Courts." *Critique of Anthropology* 32, no. 4: 388–414.

———. 2016. *Inside Rwanda's Gacaca Courts Seeking Justice after Genocide*. University of Wisconsin Press.

Israël, Leora, and Guillaume Mouralis. 2014. "Introduction." In *Dealing with Wars and Dictatorships: Legal Concepts and Categories in Action*. T.M.C. Asser Press.

Jaji, Rose. 2017. "Under the Shadow of Genocide: Rwandans, Ethnicity and Refugee Status." *Ethnicities* 17, no. 1: 47–65.

Karnavas, Michael. 2007. "Gathering Evidence in International Criminal Trials: The View of the Defence Lawyer," in *International Criminal Justice: A Critical Analysis of Institutions and Procedures*, edited by Michael Bohlander. Cameron May Ltd., 75–152.

Kelsall, Tim. 2013. *Business, Politics, and the State in Africa: Challenging the Ortho-doxies on Growth and Transformation.* Zed Books.

Kersten, Mark. 2015. "Why the ICC Won't Prosecute Museveni." *Justice in Conflict.* March 19, at https://justiceinconflict.org/2015/03/19/why-the-icc-wont-prose cute-museveni/

———. 2019. "Some Quick Reflections on the Gbagbo Acquittal at the ICC." *Justice in Conflict.* January 18, at https://justiceinconflict.org/2019/01/18/some-quick -reflections-on-the-gbagbo-acquittal-at-the-icc/.

Kiir, Salva, and Riek Machar. 2016. "Opinion: South Sudan Needs Truth, Not Trials," *New York Times,* June 7.

Kindersley, Nicki. 2019. "Rule of Whose Law? The Geography of Authority in Juba, South Sudan." *Journal of Modern African Studies* 57, no. 1: 61–83.

Kindersley, Nicki, and Øystein H. Rolandsen. 2017. "Civil War on a Shoestring: Rebellion in South Sudan's Equatoria Region." *Civil Wars* 19, no. 3: 308–24.

Klabbers, Jan. 2015. *An Introduction to International Institutional Law.* Cambridge University Press.

Knopf, Kate Almquist. 2016. *Ending South Sudan's Civil War.* Council on Foreign Relations.

Koskenniemi, Martti. 2005. *From Apology to Utopia. The Structure of International Legal Argument.* Cambridge University Press.

Kritz, Neil J. 1995. *Transitional Justice: How Emerging Democracies Reckon with Former Regimes,* vol. 1. U.S. Institute for Peace.

Labuda, Patryk I. 2017. "Taking Complementarity Seriously: Why Is the Interna-tional Criminal Court Not Investigating Government Crimes in Congo?" April 28, at http://opiniojuris.org/2017/04/28/33093/.

Lingaas, Carola. 2020. *The Concept of Race in International Criminal Law.* Routledge.

Logan, Sarah. 2017. "Why Elections Matter for Democracy in Africa. The Cases of Kenya and Rwanda." *The Conversation.* August 3, at https://theconversation.com /why-elections-matter-for-democracy-in-africa-the-cases-of-kenya-and-rwanda -82013.

Maison, Rafaëlle, and Géraud de Geouffre de La Pradelle. 2014. "L'ordonnance du juge Bruguière comme objet négationniste." *Cités 2014/1,* no. 57: 79–90, at www .cairn.info/revue-cites-2014-1-page-79.htm#no3.

Mamdani, Mahmood. 1996. *Citizen and Subject: Contemporary Africa and the Legacy of Late Colonialism.* Princeton University Press.

———. 2002. *When Victims Become Killers: Colonialism, Nativism, and the Genocide in Rwanda.* Princeton University Press.

Massoud, Mark. 2013. *Law's Fragile State: Colonial, Authoritarian and Humanitarian Legacies in Sudan.* Cambridge University Press.

May, Larry. 2010. *Genocide: A Normative Account.* Cambridge University Press.

Mbeki, Thabo, and Mahmood Mamdani. 2014. "Opinion: Courts Can't End Civil Wars." *New York Times.* February 5.

Mednick, Sam. 2019. "South Sudan Turns to Tourism in a Bid to Draw Line under

Past Unrest." *The Guardian.* September 6, www.theguardian.com/global-devel
opment/2019/sep/06/south-sudan-turns-to-tourism-in-bid-to-draw-line-under
-past-unrest.

Melvern, Linda. 2006. *A People Betrayed: The Role of the West in Rwanda's Genocide; Conspiracy to Murder.* Verso.

———. 2020. *Intent to Deceive: Denying the Rwandan Genocide.* Verso.

Melvern, Linda, and others. 2014. "BBC Genocide Film: Protest Letter by 38 Inter-national Researchers and Historians." *The New Times.* October 12, www.new times.co.rw/section/read/181969.

———. 2018. "Rebuttal to 'NGO Justice: African Rights as Pseudo-Prosecutor of the Rwandan Genocide.'" *Human Rights Quarterly* 40, no. 2: 447–65.

Meredith, Martin. 2003. *Mugabe: Power, Plunder, and the Struggle for Zimbabwe.* PublicAffairs.

Mettraux, Guénaël. 2008. "Judicial Inheritance: The Value and Significance of the Nuremberg Trial to Contemporary War Crimes Tribunals." In *Perspectives on the Nuremberg Trial,* edited by Guénaël Mettraux. Oxford University Press.

Milmo, Cahal. 2008. "Mastermind behind Rwanda Genocide Jailed for Life." *Inde-pendent.* December 19, www.independent.co.uk/news/world/africa/mastermind -behind-rwanda-genocide-jailed-for-life-1203697.html.

Minear, Richard. 1971. *Victors' Justice: Tokyo War Crimes Trial.* Princeton University Press.

Mitchell, Michelle, and Nick Louvel, directors. 2015. *The Uncondemned* (documen-tary film), at www.imdb.com/title/tt4082346/.

Moro, Leben Nelson. 2006. "Oil, War and Forced Migration in Sudan." *St Antony's International Review* 2, no. 1: 75–90

Nouwen, Sarah. 2013. *Complementarity in the Line of Fire: The Catalysing Effect of the International Criminal Court in Uganda and Sudan.* Cambridge University Press.

Off, Carol. 2001. *The Lion, the Fox and the Eagle.* Vintage Canada.

Ohlin, Jens. 2009. "Towards a Unique Theory of International Criminal Sentenc-ing." In *International Criminal Procedure: Towards a Coherent Body of Law,* edited by Göran Sluiter and Sergey Vasiliev. Cameron May.

Okuk, James. 2018. "Historical Hints on Survival and Collapse Governments: Les-sons for South Sudan and IGAD-Led HLRF." *Paanluel Wël.* May 18, https://pa anluelwel.com/2018/05/17/historical-hints-on-survival-and-collapse-govern ments-lessons-for-south-sudan-and-igad-led-hlrf/.

Olsen, Tricia D., Leigh A. Payne, and Andrew G. Reiter. 2010. *Transitional Justice In Balance: Comparing Processes, Weighing Efficacy.* U.S. Institute of Peace.

Open Society Justice Initiative. 2015. "Human Rights Decisions of the East African Court of Justice." May, www.justiceinitiative.org/uploads/8e03c4f9-2950-484b -96a2-be903b9665e8/case-digests-eacj-20150526.pdf.

Overy, Richard 2003. "The Nuremberg Trials: International Law in the Making." In *From Nuremberg to the Hague,* edited by Phillipe Sands. Cambridge University Press.

Palmer, Nicola. 2015. *Courts in Conflict: Interpreting the Layers of Justice in Post-genocide Rwanda.* Oxford University Press.

Peskin, Victor. 2005. "Beyond Victor's Justice? The Challenge of Prosecuting the Winners at the International Criminal Tribunals for the Former Yugoslavia and Rwanda." *Journal of Human Rights* 4 (April): 213–31.

———. 2008. *International Justice in Rwanda and the Balkans: Virtual Trials and the Struggle for State Cooperation.* Cambridge University Press.

———. 2009. "Caution and Confrontation in the International Criminal Court's Pursuit of Accountability in Uganda and Sudan." *Human Rights Quarterly* 31, no. 3: 655–91.

del Ponte, Carla, with Chuck Sudetic. 2009. *Madame Prosecutor Confrontations with Humanity's Worst Criminals and the Culture of Impunity: A Memoir.* Other Press.

Primus, Richard. 1996. "A Brooding Omnipresence: Totalitarianism in Postwar Constitutional Thought." *Yale Law Journal* 106, no. 2: 423–57.

Possi, Ally. 2016. "It's Official: The East African Court of Justice Can Now Adjudicate Human Rights Cases." *AfriLaw Blog.* February, at https://africlaw.com/2016/02/01/its-official-the-east-african-court-of-justice-can-now-adjudicate-human-rights-cases/#more-1048.

———. 2017. "The Draconian Time Limitation Clause against Private Litigants of the East African Court of Justice: A Commentary on Steven Dennis Case." *iCourts Working Paper Series,* no. 103. University of Copenhagen.

Prosperi, Luigi, and Jacopo Terrosi. 2017. "Embracing the 'Human Factor': Is There New Impetus at the ICC for Conceiving and Prioritizing Intentional Environmental Harms as Crimes Against Humanity?" *Journal of International Criminal Justice* 15, no. 3 (July): 509–25.

Prunier, Gérard. 2010. *Africa's World War: Congo, The Rwanda Genocide, and the Making of a Continental Catastrophe.* Oxford University Press.

Quinn, Joanna. 2009. *Reconciliation(s): Transitional Justice in Postconflict Societies.* McGill-Queen's University Press.

Rever, Judi. 2018. *In Praise of Blood: The Crimes of the Rwandan Patriotic Front.* Penguin Random House.

Reydams, Luc. 2016. "NGO Justice: African Rights as Pseudo-Prosecutor of the Rwandan Genocide." *Human Rights Quarterly* 38, no. 3: 547–88.

Reyntjens, Filip. 2009. *The Great African War: Congo and Regional Geopolitics, 1996–2006.* Cambridge University Press.

———. 2014. "Rwanda's Untold Story. A Reply to '38 Scholars, Scientists, Researchers, Journalists and Historians.'" *African Arguments.* October 21, https://africanarguments.org/2014/10/rwandas-untold-story-a-reply-to-38-scholars-scientists-researchers-journalists-and-historians-by-filip-reyntjens/.

Robinson, Darryl. 2013. "International Criminal Law as Justice." *Journal of International Criminal Justice* 11, no. 3: 699–711. https://doi-org.proxy1-bib.sdu.dk/10.1093/jicj/mqt039.

Robinson, Mary. 2004. "Foreword." In *The Princeton Principles on Universal Jurisdiction,* edited by Stephen Macedo. Princeton University Press.

Rohan, Colleen, and Gentian Zyberi, eds. 2018. *Defense Perspectives on International Criminal Justice.* Cambridge University Press.

Rolandsen, Øystein H. 2011. "The Making of the Anya-Nya Insurgency in the Southern Sudan, 1961–64." *Journal of Eastern African Studies* 5, no. 2: 211–32.

———. 2015. "Norway's Role in South Sudan's Independence." November 27, https://blogs.prio.org/MonitoringSouthSudan/2015/11/norways-role-in-south-sudans-independence/.

Röling, Bert V., and Antonio Cassese. 1993. *The Tokyo Trial and Beyond.* Polity Press.

Roth, Brad. 2010. "Coming to Terms with Ruthlessness: Sovereign Equality, Global Pluralism, and the Limits of International Criminal Justice." *Santa Clara Journal of International Law* 231, no. 8.

Rovetta, Ornella. 2014. "Le procès de Jean-Paul Akayesu. Les autorités communales en jugement." *Vingtième Siècle. Revue d'histoire* 122: 51–61.

Ryngaert, Cedric. 2013. "State Cooperation with the International Criminal Tribunal for Rwanda." *International Criminal Law Review* 13.1: 125–46.

Sadat, Leila N. 2018. "Fiddling While Rome Burns? The Appeals Chamber's Curious Decision in Prosecutor v. Jean-Pierre Bemba Gombo." *EJIL: Talk!* (blog, *European Journal of International Law*). June 12, www.ejiltalk.org/fiddling-while-rome-burns-the-appeals-chambers-curious-decision-in-prosecutor-v-jean-pierre-bemba-gombo/.

———. 2019. "Why the ICC's Judgment in the al Bashir Case Wasn't So Surprising." *Just Security.* July 12, www.justsecurity.org.

Savelsberg, Joachim. 2015. *Representing Mass Violence: Conflicting Responses to Human Rights Violations in Darfur.* University of California Press.

Schabas, William A. 2003. "National Courts Finally Begin to Prosecute Genocide, the Crime of Crimes." *Journal of International Criminal Justice* 1, no. 39: 39–63.

———. 2008. "Unexplained (and Unacceptable) Delays at the International Criminal Tribunal for Rwanda." November 2, http://humanrightsdoctorate.blogspot.com/2008/11/unexplained-and-unacceptable-delays-at.html.

Scheingold, Stuart A. 2004. *The Politics of Rights: Lawyers, Public Policy, and Political Change.* University of Michigan Press.

Scott, James C. 1999. *Seeing Like a State: How Certain Schemes to Improve the Human Condition Have Failed.* Yale University Press.

Segal, Aaron. 1965. "Reviewed Work(s): *East African Unity through Law* by Thomas M. Franck; *Federation in East Africa* by C. Leys and P. Robson; *Pan-Africanism and East African Integration* by Joseph S. Nye Jr." *Journal of Modern African Studies* 3, no. 4 (December): 633–35, at www.jstor.org/stable/pdf/159194.pdf?refreqid=excelsior%3A06bc908e489d00ef4f5ddbefab6ba93d.

Shany, Yuval. 2014. *Assessing the Effectiveness of International Courts.* Oxford University Press.

Shapiro, Martin. 1981. *Courts: A Comparative and Political Analysis.* University of Chicago Press.

Sharp, Dustin N. 2018. *Rethinking Transitional Justice for the Twenty-First Century: Beyond the End of History.* Cambridge University Press.

Sikkink, Kathryn. 2011. *The Justice Cascade: How Human Rights Prosecutions Are Changing World Politics.* W. W. Norton & Company.

de Silva, Nicole, and Anne Holthoefer. 2019. "The Power of Legal Norm Entrepreneurs in Legalization Processes: Lessons from the United Nations' and African Union's Development of International Criminal Law." Presented at the International Studies Association Annual Convention, Toronto, March 27–30.

Sirleaf, Matiangai. 2017. "The African Justice Cascade and the Malabo Protocol." *International Journal of Transitional Justice* 11, no. 1 (March): 71–91.

Stewart, Catrina. 2013. "ICC on Trial along with Kenya's Elite amid Claims of Bribery and Intimidation." *The Guardian*, October 1, www.theguardian.com/world/2013/oct/01/icc-trial-kenya-kenyatta-ruto.

Straus, Scott. 2006. *The Order of Genocide: Race, Power, and War in Rwanda.* Cornell University Press.

Stys, Patrycja. 2012. "Revisiting Rwanda." *Journal of Modern African Studies* 50: 707–20.

Subotic, Jelena. 2013. *Hijacked Justice: Dealing with the Past in the Balkans.* Cornell Univerity Press.

Sundaram, Anjan. 2016. *Bad News: Last Journalists in a Dictatorship.* Anchor.

Taye, Mihreteab Tsighe. 2018. "International Courts in the Context of Region Building: An Analysis of the Creation and Institutionalization of the EACJ and SADC." PhD dissertation, University of Copenhagen, September 2018.

———. 2020. "Human Rights, the Rule of Law and the East African Court of Justice: Lawyers and the Emergence of a Weak Regional Field." *iCourts Working Paper Series*, no. 189. University of Copenhagen.

Teitel, Ruti G. 2000. *Transitional Justice.* Oxford University Press.

Teubner, Gunther. 2015. "Exogenous Self-Binding: How National and International Courts Contribute to Transnational Constitutionalization." In *Transconstitutionalism*, edited by G. F. da Fonseca and M. A. L. L. deBarros. Ashgate.

Thomson, Susan. 2018. *Rwanda: From Genocide to Precarious Peace.* Yale University Press.

Thulliez, Henri. 2020. "Prosecutions in Chad." In *The President on Trial: Prosecuting Hissène Habré*, edited by Sharon Weill, Kim Thuy Seelinger, and Kerstin Bree Carlson. Oxford University Press.

de Tocqueville, Alexis. 2002. *Democracy in America*, translated, edited, and with an Introduction by Harvey C. Mansfield and Delba Winthrop. University of Chicago Press.

Toïngar, Ésaïe. 2006. *A Teenager in the Chad Civil War: A Memoir of Survival, 1982–1986.* MacFarland.

Uwera, Ange. 2017. "President Kagame Is One of the 10 Richest Presidents in Africa." *Le Rwaindais.* November 26, www.lerwandais.com/president-kagame -one-10-richest-presidents-africa/.

Van Schaak, Beth. 2008. "Engendering Genocide: The *Akayesu* Case Before the International Criminal Tribunal for Rwanda." *Santa Clara Law Commons*, at https://digitalcommons.law.scu.edu/cgi/viewcontent.cgi?article=1626&context= facpubs.

Vidal, Claudine. 2018. "Debate: Judi Rever Will Not Let Anything Stand in the Way of Her Quest to Document a Second Rwandan Genocide." *The Conversation.* September 11, http://theconversation.com/debate-judi-rever-will-not-let-any thing-stand-in-the-way-of-her-quest-to-document-a-second-rwandan-genocide -98662.

Wacquant, Loïc. 2009. *Punishing the Poor: The Neoliberal Government of Social Insecurity.* Duke University Press.

Weber, Max. 2013. "Politics as a Vocation." In *The Vocation Lectures*, edited by David Owen and Tracy B. Strong, translated by Rodney Livingstone. Hackett.

Weill, Sharon, Kim Thuy Seelinger, and Kerstin Bree Carlson, eds. 2020. *The President on Trial: Prosecuting Hissène Habré.* Oxford University Press.

White, Tom. 2018. "States 'Failing to Seize Sudan's Dictator Despite Genocide Charge.'" *The Guardian.* October 21, www.theguardian.com/global-development /2018/oct/21/omar-bashir-travels-world-despite-war-crime-arrest-warrant.

Williams, Sarah. 2016. *Hybrid and Internationalised Criminal Tribunals: Selected Jurisdictional Issues.* Hart Publishing.

Wrong, Michela. 2019. "South Africa 'Covering up Murder of ex-Rwandan Spy Boss." *The Guardian.* January 16, www.theguardian.com/world/2019/jan/16/ death-ex-rwandan-spy-boss-was-political-killing-inquest-told-patrick-karegeya.

———. 2021. *Do Not Disturb: The Story of a Political Murder and an African Regime Gone Bad.* Public Affairs Books.

Recommended Reading

Introduction

Martin Shapiro, in *Courts: A Comparative and Political Analysis* (University of Chicago Press, 1981), began a field of inquiry into the structural politics of courts, showing how they are legitimized by a series of myths about how they work that they cannot in fact achieve.

Alexander M. Bickel, *The Morality of Consent* (Yale University Press, 1975), has written a short tour de force that outlines the contradictions inherent in constitutional systems between rights and politics.

Stuart Scheingold, *The Politics of Rights: Lawyers, Public Policy, and Political Change*, 2nd ed. (University of Michigan Press, 2004), is the basis for sociological legal scholarship. Scheingold identifies that constitutional rule of law is founded in a "myth of rights" that imagines that courts can articulate and protect rights.

Robert Cover considers the structural violence inherent in law even as it proclaims itself neutral. His two most famous articles are "Violence and the Word" and "Nomos and Narrative," from his book *Justice Accused: Antislavery and the Judicial Process* (Yale University Press, 1984).

Nicola Lacey and R. Anthony Duff are both producing contemporary theory about the social function of criminal law. For Duff, this relates to its communicative function: see *Punishment, Communication and Community* (Oxford University Press, 2001). Lacey traces how social function and legal doctrine interact and evolve: see *In Search of Criminal Responsibility: Ideas, Interests, and Institutions* (Oxford University Press, 2016).

Chapter 1

On the history of the development of international criminal law:

From Nuremberg to the Hague, edited by Philippe Sands (Cambridge University Press, 2003), is a short and quick-read book. Five chapters explore five international law greats: Richard Overy, Cherie Booth, Andrew Clapham, James Crawford, and Sands himself. All are professors and authors of leading international law textbooks. The chapters are based on lectures sponsored by *The Guardian* newspaper, accessible and fascinating.

Perspectives on the Nuremberg Trials, edited by Guénaël Mettraux (Oxford University Press, 2008), is a hefty, definitive volume of contemporaneous and retrospective essays on the tribunal from leading thinkers and practitioners, edited by a practicing international criminal defense lawyer and academic.

Michael R. Marrus, *The Nuremberg War Crimes Trial 1945–46: A Documentary History* (Bedford/St. Martin's Press, 1997), excerpts key documents surrounding the creation, function, and politics of the Nuremberg Tribunals.

On the transitional justice function of international criminal courts:

Lawrence Douglas, *The Memory of Judgment: Making Law and History in Trials of the Holocaust* (Yale University Press, 2001), tells the story of how lawyers used the constraints and possibilities of legal doctrine and process to develop a narrative of the Holocaust.

Donald Bloxham, *Genocide on Trial: War Crimes Trials and the Formation of Holocaust History and Memory* (Oxford University Press, 2001), offers a remarkable, rigorous investigation connecting the specifics of postwar trials to the facts that emerged as the history of the period.

On the creation and work of the ICC:

William Schabas offers a view of the International Criminal Court that is both academic and lively. It is a classic not to be missed, now in its sixth edition: *An Introduction to the International Criminal Court* (Cambridge University Press, 2020).

Witnesses and their testimony constitute huge, unresolved problems for international criminal courts. Nancy Combs's fascinating *Fact-Finding without Facts: The Uncertain Evidentiary Foundations of International Criminal Convictions* (Cambridge University Press, 2010) follows the problems of evidence gathering and presentation before the ICC. Small and mobile, ICC operatives and investigators can never hope to attain local expertise and are thus eternally at the mercy of local operators and their interests. This makes the information they collect particularly subjective.

Sarah Nouwen's *Complementarity in the Line of Fire: The Catalysing Effect of the International Criminal Court in Uganda and Sudan* (Cambridge University Press, 2014) examines the domestic impact, in Sudan and Uganda, of ICC investigations. Her lively, anthropological account finds the investigations reverberate but do not increase domestic commitment to prosecuting atrocities.

On the ICC and African law and politics:

Peter Brett and Line Engbo Gissel's *Africa and the Backlash Against International Courts* (Zed Books, 2020) digs into the complexity of sovereignty to show how backlash against international justice is rooted in broader legitimation strategies African states engage.

Similarly, Phil Clark, *Distant Justice: The Impact of the International Criminal Court on African Politics* (Cambridge University Press, 2018), and M. Kamari Clarke,

Fictions of Justice: The International Criminal Court and the Challenge of Legal Plural-
ism in Sub-Sahara Africa (Cambridge University Press, 2009), consider how the ICC
impacts politics across several African states.

Chapter 2

Philip Gourevitch's *We Wish to Inform You that Tomorrow We Will be Killed with*
Our Families (Farrar, Straus and Giroux, 1998) is one of the first books written on the
particulars of the Rwandan genocide and remains an extraordinary consideration.

Gérard Prunier's *Africa's World War* (Oxford University Press, 2009) is a thorough, impeccably researched masterpiece tracing how the conflict in Rwanda has
contributed to political unrest and mass violence in several African countries.

Susan Thomson's *Rwanda: From Genocide to Precarious Peace* (Yale University
Press, 2018) provides the latest, very thorough challenge to the popular wisdom of
Rwanda's recovery.

Helen Epstein's *Another Fine Mess: America, Uganda and the War on Terror* (Co-
lumbia Global Reports, 2017) situates Rwanda's political pressures within the wider
context of east Africa, specifically Uganda. Epstein's accessible style and devastating
critique make complex and unfamiliar east African politics digestible and suitably
chilling.

Rene Lemarchand's "Reconsidering France's Role in the Rwanda Genocide"
(June 13, 2018) is a non-paywalled article published on the website Africa Is a Country. It situates the politics and debates regarding the politics of facts in Rwanda
against a global backdrop and is available at https://africasacountry.com/2018/06/re
considering-frances-role-in-the-rwandan-genocide.

Chapter 3

For more detail regarding how Habré was brought before the CAE, see Sharon
Weill, Kim Thuy Seelinger, and Kerstin Bree Carlson's *The President on Trial: Pros-*
ecuting Hissène Habré (Oxford University Press, 2020).

Regarding hybrid justice, see Kirsten Ainley and Mark Kersten, *Dakar Guidelines*
on the Establishment of Hybrid Courts (LSE & Wayamo Foundation, 2019) at http://
eprints.lse.ac.uk/101134/1/Dakar_Guidelines_print_version_corr_1_.pdf, and
Aaron Fichtelberg's *Hybrid Tribunals: A Comparative Examination* (Routledge 2015).

Regarding universal jurisdiction, Brad Roth's "Coming to Terms with Ruthlessness: Sovereign Equality, Global Pluralism, and the Limits of International Criminal
Justice," *Santa Clara Journal of International Law* 8 (2009), presents a conclusive and
damning assessment of its limitations.

Chapter 4

Kate Almquist Knopf's *Ending South Sudan's Civil War* (Council on Foreign Relations, 2016) is a short and direct summary of how fracturing power and eroding
social structures makes any eventual peace more difficult.

In *What Is the What* (Penguin, 2006), Dave Eggers recounts the biographical story of Valentino Achak Deng, who became a child refugee and later was brought to the United States as one of Sudan's "lost boys." Eggers interviewed Deng and wrote this account of his refugee journey beginning in Sudan in the 1980s and across East Africa before arriving in Atlanta, Georgia. Deng later returned to South Sudan and opened a school for girls. Proceeds from the book go to support the school. See www .vadfoundation.com/.

Mark Massoud, *Law's Fragile State: Colonial, Authoritarian and Humanitarian Legacies in Sudan* (Cambridge University Press, 2013), describes legal authority in Sudan over the past hundred years, showing how varying elites have used law to further their projects and interests. The book challenges assumptions that Sudan has been "lawless" during this time and also debates the idea that law is a force that serves primarily democratic, human rights–based interests.

Nicki Kindersley, "Rule of Whose law? The Geography of Authority in Juba, South Sudan," *Journal of Modern African Studies* 57, no. 1: 61–83, provides an excellent examination of how governance works and what it looks like on the ground in South Sudan.

Tim Kelsall, *Business, Politics, and the State in Africa: Challenging the Orthodoxies on Growth and Transformation* (Zed Books, 2013), makes a compelling argument for rethinking how authority is practiced in developing states.

Chapter 5

If you are looking for sources that examine the EACJ in greater detail, I suggest three works:

Karen J. Alter, James T. Gathii, and Laurence R. Helfer, "Backlash against International Courts in West, East and Southern Africa: Causes and Consequences," *European Journal of International Law* 27, no. 2 (2016): 293–328.

Emmanuel Ugirashebuja, John Eudes Ruhangisa, Tom Ottervanger, and Armin Cuyvers, eds., *East African Community Law: Institutional, Substantive and Comparative EU Aspects* (Brill, 2017).

Ally Possi, "An Appraisal of the Functioning and Effectiveness of the East African Court of Justice," *Potchefstroom Electronic Law Journal* 21, no. 1 (2018).

Conclusion

For more international and African discussions of African issues, in English, I recommend perusing the African Arguments series published by Zed Books and subscribing to the website Africa Is a Country at https://africasacountry.com/.

Index

www.ingramcontent.com/pod-product-compliance
Lightning Source LLC
Chambersburg PA
CBHW022320280326
41932CB00010B/1165